D0810701

CONCEPT DEVELOPMENT

AND THE

DEVELOPMENT OF

THE GOD CONCEPT

IN THE CHILD:

A BIBLIOGRAPHY

V. Peter Pitts

Foreword by John H. Peatling

Character Research Press
207 State Street
Schenectady, New York 12305 U.S.A.

CONTENTS

International Standard Book Number 0-915744-07-4
Library of Congress Catalog Card No. L. C. 77-70266
First Printing

© Ernest M. Ligon 1977

CONCEPT DEVELOPMENT AND THE DEVELOPMENT OF THE GOD CONCEPT IN THE CHILD: A BIBLIOGRAPHY

EDITOR'S FOREWORD:

Humans are amazing. To some Love, Country, Courage, Kindness are realities. To others, G-O-D is a three-letter word indicative of a similar or, even, supra-reality. However, for some humans if a thing cannot be pinched, punched, held, or cut apart it is not "real." At some ages Santa, fairies, goblins, and demons are very real. At other (usually later) ages, most of these "realities" assume some other form: often they simply fade into unreality.

None of this is exactly news. Most humans on the late side of adolescence accept these facts. Therefore, the shift from reality to reality is merely one more "fact of life." That is really too bad. An easy acceptance of this shift causes all too many to ignore that shift in realities, to withdraw their curiosity from one of the most persistent and amazing phenomena of human living, the progressive construction and re-construction of that reality within which one lives out the years of his life.

A particularly important instance of this phenomenon in a theistic culture is the development of a concept of God during the process of "growing up." Adults "know" that one *cannot* "see" God: at least, most adults know that! But that does not stop many of them from presuming God's "reality," or from crediting God with a sometimes remarkably diverse set of actions. Children do not start their lives "knowing" any such thing. But somehow they "learn" that fact. The amazing thing is that they learn that fact and, yet, many still grant a form of "reality" to that God who is unseeable, untouchable, unpinchable, unpunchable, and indivisible. Unless one's curiosity has quite dried up, a consideration of that phenomenon should intrigue one.

V. Peter Pitts, a young North American scholar, is exploring the development of the God concept in children through a remarkably rich research technique that was last systematically used thirty years ago by Ernest Harms. Pitts' initial explorations of the pictures children draw of God indicates that the technique can permit one to discern differences among children of different ages and among children from different "religious" communities. His research has promise, for it seems to address that intriguing shift in concepts which is involved in a reconstruction of reality and, so, helps us to understand humans better. In preparation for an extensive research program to map out this "conceptual development," he created this extensive bibliography and organized it into a series of topical sections. Undoubtedly the bibliography will help him in his own research. Yet, it may do more.

Pitts' bibliography may also help others whose curiosity, interest or work brings them to the question of conceptual development. In all likelihood it will do so, if the development of a God concept is recognized as an acute example of a very general phenomenon, the progressive construction of reality. Because this possibility seems likely, the Character Research Press takes pleasure in publishing what may be a fundamental research tool.

Persons interested in religion and religious education should find this extensive bibliography a useful tool. It records a good bit of the research done in religious education over the last 75 years. Thus, it permits one to escape reinventing the inclined plane or rediscovering the wheel. It will permit much more than that! It can enable **persons** in these later years of the Twentieth Century to build upon the thinking, the theorizing, and the research of those who have gone before them. In addition, it may well help them to acknowledge the work of persons in a diversity of disciplines and, so, to create "new" and genuinely interdisciplinary knowledge.

Not so obviously, persons whose interests are not "religious" can also benefit from this tool. Whether their interest is the complex of human development, or the more specialized field of conceptual growth and development, perhaps they can find in the following pages a useful tool. At least, these entries may help some to avoid the stupidity of the *un*conscious replication. Hopefully it will do more. It may, for example, permit some to follow their curiosity to a point where they discover genuinely "new" things about human development, beginning with this instance of our ability to create a reality beyond the one known so well in childhood.

In that case, in addition to religious educators, theologians, and parish clergy, one might anticipate that psychologists, sociologists, anthropologists, counsellors, and clinicians, plus others concerned with child development, will find this bibliography to be a useful tool. One might even anticipate that the extent and depth of this work might stimulate interdisciplinary studies of the progressive construction of realities, using the God concept as a key phenomenon for the more general, broader topic of study.

A condensed version of the author's lengthy 1975 report on his early exploratory work can be found in the journal, *Character Potential: A Record of Research* (Volume 8, No. 1, November, 1976). There, under the title, "Drawing the Invisible: Children's Conceptualizations of God," Pitts describes what can be discovered at the very beginning of a careful program of research into one aspect of the progressive construction of reality. As that program progresses, one can hope to hear more from this young scholar. One can also hope that his work will give to those interested in the topic not only information but further tools for their own work. Most particularly, one can hope to receive a standardized analytical procedure for dealing with a rich source of information, the artistic creations of children.

In his own Author's Preface, the ideal of an intellectual Village Green is stressed. One need not be a sociologist (as the author is) to respond positively to that ideal. Perhaps all that is necessary is a *recognition* that others address the same or similar problems, but do so from different perspectives, beginning with "other" presumptions, working within "other" theoretical contexts, yet contributing to knowledge about one's own problem. For some that recognition may be quite easy, while for others there may be veritable mountains of prejudice to cross before it can be achieved. Whatever the effort, the possibility of learning from others, of building upon past work toward new discoveries, of discussing common concerns, of improving one's own work, makes the ideal appealing. Perhaps scholars and practitioners may yet discuss their common problems, exchange their varying insights, and share their separate discoveries.

Since 1935 the Union College Character Research Project has probed human development from birth through childhood to adolescence. From the beginning, Value and Judgement have been recognized as important aspects of the personality that is progressively shaped by living and learning. The concept of God has been, for many of those who have been studied across the years, one of the important values. Therefore, for many years the Project has discerned the effect of what this young scholar has set out to describe. That may well be why it is with such pleasure that the Character Research Press publishes this bibliography. Still, the allure of Pitts' ideal of an intellectual Village Green is also real, as is the hope that this research tool will lead some toward the realization of that ideal.

JOHN H. PEATLING, Ph.D.
Director of Basic Research
Union College
    Character Research Project

AUTHOR'S PREFACE

In even this Age of Specialization social scientists all too often ignore the advantages inherent in interdisciplinary research. This is true albeit ironic in Sociology, for the early sociologists strove to make their discipline one that integrated all others into a coherent whole. Unfortunately, their ideal was never fully realized. Instead, the attempt led to a certain disciplinocentrism and an academic isolation. Sociology developed its own vocabulary, its own methods and its own theoretical orientation and, then, with these defined itself in relation to the other extant disciplines. As a result, all too little was integrated.

A General Orientation and Perspective

I have ventured outside the now traditional boundaries of Sociology. Instead of choosing a research topic amenable to current disciplinary methods and theories, I have chosen a topic and then found methods and theories amenable to it. That is my orientation as I seek to study Children's Conceptions and Artistic Representations of God through the pictures children create of God.

The study itself was born during a seminar on the Sociology of Religion at the University of Iowa during the Fall of 1974. From the perspective of a Sociology of Knowledge, perhaps it was quite probable that I should have chosen such a research topic. In my undergraduate years I developed a strong interest in an interdisciplinary approach to knowledge. My academic interests ranged from mathematics to philosophy, from art to religion. I might well have become a liberal arts major, I suppose, had I not valued a systematic, scientific method of study. When I did decide to major in Sociology, I naively assumed that it was an eclectic discipline that could integrate the common aspects of a variety of disciplines. I expected it to be a kind of intellectual Village Green where people from many disciplines could meet and discuss matters of common interest.

That I did not discover what I expected did not stop me. Instead, I have become more and more intrigued by the multiple relationships among Religion, Learning Theory, Developmental Psychology, Educational Psychology, and Child Art. The result is my study of the pictures that children draw of God.

It is my hope that my work may be an invitation to such an intellectual Village Green. It is extremely important for people from a variety of disciplines to exchange ideas and data on the development of religious concepts. No one discipline has a corner on all that needs to be considered. Moreover, the development of religious concepts is a topic that concerns everyone. To some extent, religion is one of the main social and psychological influences in human life (at least as it is lived in the United States during these years of the late 1970s). Therefore, an attempt to understand a religion or its concepts is crucial to those who would study the human lives influenced by them.

A Brief Summary of My Research to Date

It is common knowledge that a child undergoes many changes between the ages of six and ten. He develops physically, emotionally, socially and psychologically (and in many other ways, too). The development of a God concept is an important aspect of a child's total over-all growth. But just how does one begin to discover what a child's conception of God is? And just how does one proceed to discover how a child grows into such a concept?

During the period of early childhood abstract concepts (such as God!) are difficult, if not impossible, for a child to put into words. Therefore, the best way for a child to reveal his concept of God is through a medium with which he is both familiar and comfortable, and which is consistent with his stage of mental growth, such as drawing. Thus, the analysis of the pictures of God that are drawn by children appears to give us adults our best chance of learning about children's actual conceptions of God. Moreover, it is a method that seems to be peculiarly compatible with the mental growth of the child between six and ten years of age.

During the period 1974-1976 I have been asking children from a variety of denominational backgrounds to draw pictures of God. My analyses of the 180 pictures I have collected strongly suggest that a child's conception of God changes across the age levels in a Piagetian fashion. For example, the shift from a preoperational stage to an operational stage of concrete thinking is quite evident in children's pictures of God. In fact, markedly so.

Working closely with local clergy, I collected pictures from children attending Mormon, Lutheran, Roman Catholic, Methodist, Mennonite, Jewish, and Unitarian Sunday School programs in Iowa City, Iowa. These pictures were analyzed both objectively and subjectively. For instance, they were each analyzed for their anthropomorphic and for their abstract qualities, for the amount of symbolism used, and for the overall relationship between the elements of the picture and the formal theology of their denominational background. One result of this collection and analysis was a paper that I presented at the 1975 Convention of the Religious Education Association in Philadelphia, Pennsylvania, in November of 1975. This paper, "Children's Conceptions and Artistic Representations of God: An Interdenominational Study," represented my initial attempt to take an interdisciplinary look at children's conceptions of God. In doing that, I found I had to examine ten important aspects of conceptual development.

Those ten were:

1. The *socialization processes* involved;
2. The *anthropomorphic limits* of human conceptualization and representation;
3. A *theory of symbolization;*
4. The various *social and psychological influences* on the process of conceptualization itself;
5. An integration of various *developmental theories;*

6. A comparison of the intellectualistic and perceptual *theories of Child Art;*
7. The development of *measures of anthropomorphism* in a child's drawing (my A-scores);
8. The development of *measures of the proportion of religious to non-religious elements* in a child's drawing (my Q-scores);
9. The placement of various denominations onto a *three-by-five paradigm,* for the purpose of comparing God concepts and formal denominational emphases;
10. The use of the pictures to *demonstrate and clarify both denominational differences and the stages of conceptual development.*

The last of these ten aspects, the demonstration and clarification of both denominational differences and the stages of conceptual development, has been and is a consistent interest of mine. The identification of both interdenominational and age-level differences among the children's picture of God has specified a number of questions-in-search-of-an-answer. Five major questions seem to fall into that category:

1. *What are* children's beliefs?
2. *When do* the children's beliefs & concepts *begin* to take form?
3. *How do* belief "systems" *develop?*
4. *Why do* children *believe* in God?
5. To what *extent do* childhood *experiences* with the concept of God strengthen, negate, or change a person's *beliefs* in *adulthood?*

The study of Children's Conceptions and Artistic Representations of God is, I hope, but the *first phase* in a lengthy program of research that will, eventually, include designs appropriate to these five questions. Thus, my present study is intended to be a foundation for a program of continuing research on children's conceptual development. At this time (late 1976), possible future research could profitably include studies of any one (or all!) of the following eight topics:

1. The God concepts of children who are *not* exposed to *any* "formal" program of religious education;

2. The God concepts of children in *"different" cultures;*

3. The God concepts of children in *non-Western albeit theistic religious groups;*

4. The *conceptual development of one specific group of children* from the "first" to the "fourth" school grade level *via a longitudinal study;*

5. The *conceptual and artistic development of one individual* from birth through age eleven, *via an in-depth case study;*

6. The God concepts of children who have an opportunity to use *color* as well as, or *instead of black and white* line drawings *to picture God* (e.g., colored paper and crayons, instead of lead pencils on white paper);

7. The God concepts of children of identifiable *racial or ethnic minorities;*

8. The God concepts of children of parents belonging to *Christian "fundamentalist" groups,* or of children in any area of the United States with many such groups (e.g., children in Eastern Kentucky and/or in Western West Virginia).

So far, my studies of children's pictures of God have been almost entirely exploratory and descriptive in nature; yet they seem to have stimulated a considerable amount of interest. During the Fall of 1975 I reported on my work at two conferences on religious education: (a) a Family Life Conference that was held at St. Ambrose College in Davenport, Iowa (October 18, 1975), and the Convention of the Religious Education Association that was held in Philadelphia, Pennsylvania (November 23-26, 1975). An article in a diocesan newspaper, "God's Like Snoopy, a Squiggle, and Ten Fingers," also appeared in the December 18, 1975 issue of *The Catholic Messenger* of Davenport, Iowa. In addition, during 1976-1977 two articles reporting on my research are to be published: an article, "Drawing Pictures of God," is scheduled to appear in the English journal, *Learning for Living* (CEM-Annandale, 2 Chester House, Pages Lane, London, N10 1PR, U.K.), while a condensed version of my longer R. E. A. paper is scheduled to appear in the journal *Character Potential: A Record of Research* (Union College Character Research Project, 207 State Street, Schenectady, New York 12305, U.S.A.).

As I have progressed with my research I have been helped by my correspondence with a number of persons, many of whom have freely given me the benefit of their advice and encouragement. I particularly want to acknowledge the contributions of Peter Benson, Milo Brekke, David Elkind, Andre Godin, Ronald J. Goldman, P. J. Lawrence, John H. Peatling, Mary Perkins Ryan, Henry J. Simmons, Bernard Spilka, and E. Paul Torrance. Each of these persons has helped me with my studies, but what I have done is my responsibility and not theirs. However, I should be grossly amiss if I did not acknowledge their assistance in my work and, particularly, in identifying a number of the references that appear in this rather lengthy bibliography.

THE BIBLIOGRAPHY ITSELF: An Explanation, Summary and Statement of Purpose

A multi-faceted study of the development of a God concept has implications for a variety of persons. It particularly has implicit value for religious educators, but also for psychologists, sociologists and structural anthropologists, for clergy and parents, and for almost anyone interested in the development of concepts and representation. Therefore, the following Bibliography should prove to be an aid to persons interested in conceptual development in many disciplines.

The actual Bibliography contains approximately six hundred references. These are presented in twelve categories, which makes the bibliography a bit easier to use. These major categories are:

1. *The GOD CONCEPT.* These 41 references concern the evolution, nature and form of the God concept across the period from Childhood to Adulthood.
2. *CONCEPT DEVELOPMENT.* These 51 references concern the term "concept" *per se* and, more specifically, refer to the fundamental topics of perception, abstraction, and human thought processes.
3. *CHILD DEVELOPMENT and DEVELOPMENTAL CHILD PSYCHOLOGY.* These 77 references concern specific studies of the physical and mental development of the child, with an especial focus on the work of J. Piaget and other developmental psychologists.
4. *RELIGIOUS EDUCATION.* These 51 references concern the everyday problems of religious educators, with especial concern for the methods and forms of religious education appropriate for various age groups of children.
5. *Children's RELIGIOUS THOUGHT and DEVELOPMENT.* These 78 references concern *specific research* done on the subject of what can be termed "religious" conceptual development. Most of the listed references deal with "religious" development in a more theoretical manner than the references listed in Section 4 (above). For example, David Elkind's 1970 article, "The Origins of Religion in the Child," introduces a Piagetian approach to the religious development of the child that I have used. This Section of the Bibliography includes, as well, the *only previous systematic* attempts to study the God concepts of children through analyses of Child Art (i.e., the studies of Ernest Harms in the United States and that of J. E. Johnson in the United Kingdom).
6. *SYMBOLS, SIGNS and RELIGIOUS IMAGERY.* These 22 references concern the symbols, images, signs, language and behavior associated with religious concepts. Many of these references focus particularly upon the *function* of symbolism and imagery in the realm of the religious.

7. *CHILDREN'S ART and DRAW-A-"Something" TESTS.*
    These 92 references concern both historical and contem-
    porary works that deal with Children's Art. The "classi-
    cal" works by Kellogg, Goodenough, and Harris receive
    particular attention, since the method I have used to ana-
    lyze and quantify children's pictures of God is very simi-
    lar to those they used for other purposes.

8. *ARTISTIC DEVELOPMENT and PSYCHOLOGY OF
    ART.* These 15 references concern technical, abstract
    works about pictorial and symbolic representation, which
    may be necessary to "fill in" the gaps in a theory of artis-
    tic and/or conceptual development.

9. *RELIGIOUS DENOMINATIONS and Their BELIEF
    SYSTEMS.* These 18 references concern the theologies
    and the practices of particular religious groups, since it
    seems self-evident that one *must* be *aware* of a religious
    group's "belief system" *before* one generalizes about the
    relationship between children's pictures and their reli-
    gious affiliation.

10. *AESTHETICS, ART CRITICISM, and PHILOSOPHY.*
    These 35 references concern the general relation between
    Art and what we call Reality. Works in this Section con-
    cern the "roots" of aesthetics and art, and include two
    important articles by Viktor Lowenfeld on the nature of
    creative and mental activity. The historical development
    of Art can, it would appear, give one important insights
    into the actual development of artistic abilities in chil-
    dren.

11. *SOCIOLOGY, PSYCHOLOGY, and PHILOSOPHY OF
    RELIGION.* These 43 references concern what can best
    be termed sociological and psychological insights into
    the general phenomenon of "religion." As with Art, a
    study of the historical development of "religion" can, it
    seems, permit one to discern certain analogical similari-
    ties between that history and the religious growth of the
    child.

12. *MISCELLANEOUS.* These 65 references are something of a potpourri; they have some (albeit often marginal) importance in the study of God concepts, and include both reference books and works of fiction and non-fiction that seem useful in establishing a background in the general field of conceptual development.

No bibliography can ever be considered complete. This one is no different. It is an extensive albeit "select" bibliography. However, it is a good starting point for someone interested in the development across time of a God concept in people. Therefore, I hope that these references will stimulate further interest in an interdisciplinary study of this "religious" phenomenon. Should that happen, perhaps that intellectual Village Green may yet become populated with persons exchanging ideas and data. From my perspective, that would be a great thing.

V. PETER PITTS
Department of Sociology
University of Iowa
Iowa City, Iowa 52242 U.S.A.

INDEX TO
A Bibliography on Concept Development and the
Development of the God Concept in the Child

BIBLIOGRAPHY

1 The God Concept

1: 1 Babin, P. (1963/1965). "The Idea of God: Its Evolution Between the Ages of 11 and 19," *From Religious Experience to a Religious Attitude,* A. Godin (ed.), Chicago, Ill.: Loyola University Press, pp. 183-198.

1: 2 Barelli, G., G. Stickler, and J. Hermans (1963). *Contribution a l'Etude Objective de l'Attitude Envers Dieu,* Louvain.

1: 3 Baskfield, G. T. (1933). *The Idea of God in British and American Idealism.* Vol. 38 of the Catholic University of America *Studies in Sacred Theology.* Washington, D.C.: Catholic University of America.

1: 4 Benson, P. and B. Spilka. (1973). "God Image and Self Esteem," *Journal for the Scientific Study of Religion,* Vol. 12, No. 3, September.

1: 5 Burgardemeier, A. (1951). *Gott und Himmel in der Psychischen Welt der Jugend (God and Heaven in the Psychological World of the Child),* Dusseldorf: Patmos.

1: 6 Cerney, M. S. (1966). "The Development of the Concept of God in Catholic School Children," *Dissertation Abstracts* (unpublished thesis), 27 (6-AO, 1650).

1: 7 Clavier, H. (1926). *L'Idee de Dieu chez l'Enfant,* Paris: Fischbacher.

1: 8 Deconchy, J.P. (1967). *Structure Genetique de l'idee de Dieu,* Brussels: Lumen Vitae.

1: 9 Deconchy, J.P. (1967). "God and Parental Images. The Masculine and Feminine in Religious Free Associations," in *From Cry to Word,* A. Godin (ed.), Brussels: Lumen Vitae, pp. 85-94.

1:10 Deconchy, J.P. (1965). "The Idea of God: Its Emergence Between 7-16 Years," in *From Religious Experience to a Religious Attitude,* A. Godin (ed.), Chicago: Loyola, pp. 97-108.

1:11 Godin, A. and M. Halley. (1964). "Parental Images and Divine Paternity," in *From Religious Experience to a Religious Attitude,* Brussels: Lumen Vitae Press, pp. 79-110. (Also Chicago: Loyola, pp. 65-96).

1:12 Gorsuch, R.L. (1968). "The Conceptualization of God as Seen in Adjective Ratings," *Journal for the Scientific Study of Religion,*

Vol. 7, No. 1, pp. 56-64.

1:13 Gorsuch, R.L. (1967). "Dimensions of the Conceptualization of God," *International Yearbook for the Sociology of Religion*, Sonderdruck aus Band 3, Koln und Opladen: Westdeutscher Verlag.

1:14 Graebner, O.E. (1960). *Child Concepts of God*. 17th Yearbook, Lutheran Education Association, 1960.

1:15 Graebner, O.E. (1965). "God-concepts of Deaf Children," paper presented at Religious Education Association meeting.

1:16 Greene, K.G. (1934). *The Evolution of the Conception of God*, Boston: Christopher Publishing House.

1:17 Hample, S. and E. Marshall (1967). *Children's Letters to God*, Simon & Schuster.

1:18 Holmes, U.T. (1974). *To Speak of God — Theology for Beginners*, New York: Seabury.

1:19 Hutsebaut, D. (1972/3). "The Representation of God: Two Complementary Approaches," *Social Compass*, Vol. 19, No. 3, pp. 389-406.

1:20 Larson, L. and R.H. Knapp. (1964). "Sex Differences in Symbolic Conceptions of the Deity," *Journal of Projective Techniques*, Vol. 28.

1:21 MacLean, A. H. (1930). *The Idea of God in Protestant Religious Education*. New York: Teachers College.

1:22 Mailhoit, B. (1961). "And God Became a Child," *Lumen Vitae Studies in Religious Education*, Vol. 16, No. 2.

1:23 Mailhoit, B. (1961). "And God Became a Child: the Reactions of Children and Child-groups Under School Age," in *Child and Adult Before God*, Brussels: Lumen Vitae Press, pp. 99-110.

1:24 Mathias, W. D. (1943). *Ideas of God and Conduct*. New York: Columbia University Press.

1:25 Mc Dowell, J.B. (1952). "The Development of the Idea of God in the Catholic Child," *Education Research Monthly*, The Catholic University of America.

1:26 Nordberg, R.B. (1971). "Developing the Idea of God in Children," *Religious Education*, pp. 376-379.

1:27 Odoroff, M. (1970). *Teaching Your Child About God*, Winona, Minn.: St. Mary's College Press.

1:28 Simmons, H. C. (1974). "Beyond Orthodoxy and Personhood: Distortions of the Image of God," *Religious Education*, pp. 23-33.

1:29 Singer, R.E. (1959). *A Study of the God Concepts of Children in Three Suburban Religious Schools.* Ph.D. Dissertation, Northwestern University.

1:30 Spilka, B., P. Armatas, and J. Nussbaum. (1964). "The Concept of God: A Factor Analytic Approach," in *Review of Religious Research,* Vol. 6, No. 1, pp. 28-36.

1:31 Spilka, B., J. Addison, and M. Rosensohn. (1975). "Parents, Self, and God: A Test of Competing Theories of Individuals-Religion Relationships," *Review of Religious Research,* Vol. 16, No. 3, pp. 154-165.

1:32 Spilka, B., M. Rosensohn and S. Tener. (1973). *Pilot Study on the Image of God:* A paper presented at the Convention of the Rocky Mountain Psychological Association, Las Vegas, Nevada.

1:33 Strunk, O. (1959). "Perceived Relationships Between Parental and Deity Concepts," *Psychological Newsletter,* 10, pp. 222-226. (Now *Journal of Psychological Studies.*)

1:34 Van Aerde, M. (1972/3). "The Attitude of Adults Towards God," *Social Compass,* Vol. 19, No. 3, pp. 407-413.

1:35 Vereruysse, G. (1972/3). "The Meaning of God: A Factor-Analytic Study," *Social Compass,* Vol. 19, No. 3, pp. 347-364.

1:36 Vergote, A. and C. Aubert. (1972/3). "Parental Images and Representations of God," *Social Compass,* Vol. 19, No. 3, pp. 431-44.

1:37 Wack, D.J. (1968). "The Image of God in Psychotherapy, a Study of Cases," in *From Cry to Word,* A. Godin (ed.), Brussels: Lumen Vitae, 1968, pp. 95-106.

1:38 Walker, D.J.C. (1950). *A Study of Children's Conceptions of God,* Unpublished Ed. B. thesis, University of Glasgow.

1:39 White, F. P. (1970). "The God of Childhood," *Dissertation Abstracts International* (Nov.) 31, (5-B) 2973.

1:40 Williams, R. (1971). "A Theory of God-Concepts Readiness: from the Piagetian Theory of the Child Artificialism and the Origin of Religious Feeling in Children," *Religious Education,* pp. 62-66.

1:41 Wolcott, C.M. (1962). *I Can Talk with God,* New York: Abingdon.

2   Concept Development

2: 1 Abeldon, R.P. and M.J. Rosenberg. (1958). "Symbolic Psychologic: a Model of Attitudinal Cognition," *Behavioral Science*, 3, pp. 1-13.

2: 2 Andrews, E.G. (1930). "The Development of Imagination in the Preschool Child," *The University of Iowa Studies in Character*, Vol. 3, No. 4

2: 3 Anthony, S. (1940). *The Child's Discovery of Death*, London: Kegan Paul, Trench, and Truber.

2: 4 Bartlett, F. (1958). *Thinking*, London: Allen and Unwin.

2: 5 Beard, R.M. (1960). *An Investigation of Concept Formation Among Infant School Children*, unpublished Ph.D. Thesis, University of London.

2: 6 Bell, C.R. (1954). "Additional Data on Anamistic Thinking," *Scientific Monthly*, 79, pp. 67-69.

2: 7 Boehm, L. (1962). "The Development of Conscience: A Comparison of American Children of Different Mental and Socioeconomic Levels," *Child Development*, 33, pp. 565-590.

2: 8 Boehm, L. (1962). "The Development of Conscience: A Comparison of Students in Catholic Parochial Schools and in Public Schools," *Child Development*, 33, pp. 591-602.

2: 9 Braine, M. S. (1960). "Problems and Issues in the Study of Conceptional Development," Paper read at *SSRC Conference*, Dedham, Mass., April.

2:10 Braun, J. S. (1963). "Relation Between Concept Formation Ability and Reading Achievement at Three Developmental Levels," *Child Development*, Vol. 34, p. 675.

2:11 Brown, R. (1958). *Words and Things*, Glencoe, Ill.: Free Press.

2:12 Bruner, J.S. (1957). "On Perceptual Readiness," *Psychological Review*.

2:13 Bruner, J.S., et. al. (1956). *A Study of Thinking*, New York: Wiley.

2:14 Deutsche, J.M. (1937). *The Development of Children's Concepts of Causal Relations*, Minneapolis: University of Minnesota Press.

2:15 Elkind, D. (1964). "Ambiguous Pictures for Study of Perceptual Development and Learning," *Child Development*, Vol. 35 (Dec.)

2:16 Elkind, D. and L. Scott. (1962). "Studies in Perceptual Development: I. The Decentering of Perception," *Child Development*, Vol. 33.

2:17 Elkind, D. et. al., (1964). "Studies in Perceptual Development: II. Part-whole Perception," *Child Development*, Vol. 35.

2:18 Green, M.R. (1961). "Prelogical Experience: Thinking," *Studies in Art Education*, Vol. 3, No. 1, p. 66.

2:19 Hartshorne, H. and F.K. Shuttleworth. (1930). *Studies in the Nature of Character*, New York: Macmillan.

2:20 Hazlitt, V. (1930). "Children's Thinking," *British Journal of Psychology*, 20, pp. 354-361.

2:21 Heidbreeder, E. (1946). "The Attainment of Concepts," *Journal of Genetic Psychology*, Vol. 35.

2:22 Hochberg, J. (1964). *Perception*, Englewood, N.J.: Prentice-Hall.

2:23 Holt, J. (1967). *How Children Learn*, New York: Dell Press.

2:24 Honkavaara, S. (1958). "The 'Dynamic-affective' Phase in the Development of Concepts," *Journal of Psychology*, 45, pp. 11-23.

2:25 Hull, C.L. (1920). "Quantitative Aspects of the Evolution of Concepts," *Psychology Monographs*, 38.

2:26 Humphrey, G. (1952). "Abstraction and Generalisation," in *Thinking: an Introduction to Experimental Psychology*, London: Methuen.

2:27 Isaacs, S. (1929). "Critical Notes: the Child's Conception of the World, by J. Piaget," *Mind*, 38, pp. 506-513.

2:28 Johnson, B. (1938). "Development of Thought," *Child Development*, Vol. 9, No. 1.

2:29 Johnson, D.M. (1955). *The Psychology of Thought and Judgement*, New York: Harper.

2:30 Kohlberg, L. (1969). "Stage and Sequence: The Cognitive Developmental Approach to Socialization," in *Handbook of Socialization:* Theory and Research, Goslin, ed., Chicago: Rand McNally.

2:31 Lee, C.L., J. Kagan, and A. Rabson. (1963). "Influence of a Preference for Analytic Categorization Upon Concept Acquisition," *Child Development*, Vol. 34.

2:32 Madge, V. (1965). *Children in Search of Meaning*, London: S.C.M. Press.

2:33 Mott, S.M. (1954). "Concept of Mother: a Study of Four and Five Year Old Children," *Child Development*, Vol. 25.

2:34 Mott, S.M. (1936). "The Development of Concepts: a Study of

          Children's Drawings," *Child Development*, Vol. 7.

2:35 Mott, S.M. (1936). "The Development of Concepts," *Journal of Genetic Psychology*, Vol. 48.

2:36 Mott, S.M. (1939). "The Growth of An Abstract Concept," *Child Development*, Vol. 10.

2:37 Nagy, M.H. (1953). "The Representation of 'Germs' by Children," *Journal of Genetic Psychology*.

2:38 Peel, E.A. (1959). "Experimental Examination of Piaget's Schemata Concerning Children's Perception and Thinking," *British Journal of Educational Psychology*, XXIX, part 2, pp. 89-102.

2:39 Reichard, S. et. al. (1944). "The Development of Concept Formation in Children," *American Journal of Orthopsychiatry*, pp. 156-161, Vol. 14.

2:40 Russell, D.H. (1956). *Children's Thinking*, Boston: Ginn.

2:41 Serra, M.C. (1952). *How to Develop Concepts and Their Verbal Representations*, Elementary School Journal, 53.

2:42 Sherif, M. (1935). "A Study of Some Social Factors in Perception," *Archives of Psychology*, N. Y., No. 187.

2:43 Smoke, K.L. (1935). "The Experimental Approach to Concept Learning," *Psychological Review*, Vol. 42.

2:44 Solley, C.M. and G. Murphey. (1960). *Development of the Perceptual World*, New York: Basic Books, Inc.

2:45 Union College Character Research Project. (1959). *Children's Religious Concepts*, Mimeographed, Schenectady: Union College.

2:46 Vernon, M.D. (1962). *The Psychology of Perception*, Baltimore: Penguin Books.

2:47 Vinacke, W.E. (1954). "Concept Formation in Children of School Ages," *Education*, Vol. 74.

2:48 Vinacke, W.E. (1951). "The Investigation of Concept Formation," *Psychological Bulletin*, Vol. 48.

2:49 Vinacke, W.E. (1952). *The Psychology of Thinking*, New York: McGraw-Hill.

2:50 Weinstein, E.A. (1957). "Development of the Concept of Flag and the Sense of National Identity," *Child Development*, Vol. 28, No. 2.

2:51 Werner, H. and E. Kaplan. (1950). "Development of Word Meaning Through Verbal Context," *The Journal of Psychology*, Vol. 29.

3. Child Development and Developmental Child Psychology

3: 1 Anderson, J.E. (1956). "Child Development: an Historical Perspective," *Child Development*, Vol. 27.

3: 2 Ausubel, D.P. (1958). *Theory and Problems of Child Development*, New York: Grune and Stratton.

3: 3 Baldwin, J.M. (1925). *Mental Development and the Race*, London: Macmillan.

3: 4 Beth, E.W. and J. Piaget. (1966). *Mathematical Epistemology and Psychology*. (Translated from French by W. Mays). Dordrecht-Holland: D. Reidel Publishing Company, New York: Gorden and Breach Science Publishers.

3: 5 Braine, M.S. (1959). "The Ontogeny of Certain Logical Operations: Piaget's Formulation Examined by Nonverbal Methods," *Psychological Monographs*, Vol. 73, No. 5. (Whole No. 475).

3: 6 Brearly, M., and E. Hitchfield (1966). *A Guide to Reading Piaget*, New York: Shocken.

3: 7 Buhler, K. (1930). *The Mental Development of the Child*, London.

3: 8 Cameron, B. and G.A. Smith. (1965). "A Descriptive Summary of an Experiment on Animism and Artificialism in the Thinking of Selected Grade I Children," *The Alberta Journal of Educational Research*, Vol. 11, No. 3, September, pp. 154-166.

3: 9 Carpenter, T.E. (1955). "A Pilot Study for a Quantitative Investigation of Jean Piaget's Original Work on Concept-formation," *Educational Review*, 7, pp. 142-149.

3:10 Darwin, C. (1877). "A Biographical Sketch of an Infant," *Mind*, Vol. 2, pp. 285-294.

3:11 Davies, G.B. (1965). "Concrete and Formal Thinking Among a Group of Adolescent Children of Average Ability," Unpublished M. Ed. Thesis, University of Birmingham, 1965.

3:12 Elkind, D. (1961). "The Additive Composition of Classes in the Child: Piaget Replication Study III," *Journal of Genetic Psychology*, Vol. 99, pp. 51-57.

3:13 Elkind, D. (1970). *Children and Adolescents*, New York: Oxford,

3:14 Elkind, D. (1961). "Children's Discovery of the Conservation of Mass, Weight, and Volume: Piaget Replication Study II," *Journal of Genetic Psychology*, Vol. 98, pp. 219-227.

3:15 Elkind, D. (1961). "The Development of Quantitative Thinking,"

Journal of Genetic Psychology, 98: 37-46.

3:16 Elkind, D. (1964). "Discrimination, Seriation and Numeration of Size and Dimensional Differences in Young Children," *Journal of Genetic Psychology*, 104: 275-296.

3:17 Elkind, D. (ed.). (1967). *Six Psychological Studies by Jean Piaget*, New York: Random House.

3:18 Erikson, E.H. (1963). *Childhood and Society*, New York: Norton.

3:19 Erikson, E.H. (1956). "The Problem of Ego Identity," *Journal of the American Psychoanalytic Association*, 4, pp. 56-121.

3:20 Escalona, S. and G.M. Heider. (1959). *Prediction and Outcome: a Study in Child Development*, New York: Basic Books.

3:21 Flavell, J.H. (1963). *The Developmental Psychology of Jean Piaget*, New York: D. Van Nostrand Company, Inc.

3:22 Gesell, A.L. (1946). *The Child from Five to Ten*, New York: Harper and Row.

3:23 Gesell, A. and L.B. Ames. (1940). *The First Five Years*, New York: Harper and Row.

3:24 Ginsburg, H. and S. Opper (1969). *Piaget's Theory of Intellectual Development: an Introduction*, Englewood Cliffs, New Jersey: Prentice-Hall, Inc.

3:25 Hall, G.S. (1891). "The Contents of Children's Minds on Entering School," *Pedagogical Seminary*, Vol. 1, pp. 139-193.

3:26 Harris, D.B. and K.M. Lansing (1966). "Research of Jean Piaget and Its Implications for Art Education in the Elementary Schools," *Studies in Art Education*, Vol. 7 (Spring '66), pp. 33-45.

3:27 Havighurst, R.J. (1953). *Human Development and Education*, New York: Longman Green and Company.

3:28 Hogan, L. (1898). *A Study of the Child*, New York: Harper & Brothers.

3:29 Hollingworth, H.L. (1928). *Mental Growth and Decline*, New York, London: Appleton.

3:30 Huang, I. (1943). "Children's Conception of Physical Causality: A Critical Summary," *Journal of Genetic Psychology*, 63, pp. 71-121.

3:31 Hurlock, E.B. (1956). *Child Development*, New York: McGraw-Hill.

3:32 Hymes, J.L. Jr. (1963). *The Child Under Six*, Englewood Cliffs, New Jersey: Prentice-Hall, Inc.

3:33 Inhelder, B. and J. Piaget (1958). *The Growth of Logical Thinking from Childhood to Adolescence,* New York: Basic Books.

3:34 Isaacs, N. (1974). *A Brief Introduction to Piaget,* Schocken.

3:35 Isaacs, S. (1945). *Intellectual Growth in Young Children,* London: G. Routledge & Son.

3:36 Jersild, A.T. (1954). *Child Psychology* (4th ed.) New York: Prentice-Hall.

3:37 Kessen, W. (1960). "Stage and Structure in the Study of Children," Paper Read at *SSRC Conference,* Dedham, Mass., April.

3:38 Koffka, K. (1928). *The Growth of the Mind,* New York: Harcourt Brace

3:39 Lewis, M.M. (1951). *Infant Speech: a Study of the Beginnings of Language* (2nd ed.). New York: Humanities.

3:40 Maier, H.W. (1969). *Three Theories of Child Development,* New York: Harper.

3:41 McCarthy, D. (1954). "Language Development in Children," in *Manual of Child Psychology,* L. Carmichael (ed.), New York: Wiley, pp. 492-630, Second Edition.

3:42 McLean, D. (1954). "Child Development: A Generation of Research," *Child Development,* Vol. 25, No. 1.

3:43 Mead, M. (1958). *The Childhood Genesis of Sex Differences in Behavior. In Discussions in Child Development III,* Tanner, Barbel, Inhelder (eds.), New York: International Universities Press.

3:44 Mogar, M. (1960). "Children's Causal Reasoning About Natural Phenomena," *Child Development,* 31, pp. 59-65.

3:45 Moustakas, C. (1974). *The Child's Discovery of Himself,* Ballantine.

3:46 Mussen, P.H., J.J. Conger, and J. Kagen. (1963). *Child Development and Personality,* New York: Harper.

3:47 Nass, M.L. (1956). "The Effects of Three Variables on Children's Concepts of Physical Causality," *Journal of Abnormal and Social Psychology,* 53, pp. 191-196.

3:48 Ojemann, R.H. and K. Pritchett (1963). "The Role of Guided Experiences in Human Development," *Perceptual and Motor Skills,* Vol. 17.

3:49 O'Shea, M.V. (1921). *Mental Development and Education,* New York: The Macmillan Company.

3:50 Parkhurst, H. (1951). *Exploring the Child's World,* New York.

3:51 Peel, E.A. (1961). *The Pupil's Thinking,* London: Oldbourne Press.

3:52 Penrod, W.T., Jr. (1964). "Approaches to the Understanding of Human Development," *Character Potential: A Record of*

Research, Vol. 2.

3:53 Piaget, J. (1952). *The Child's Conception of Number*, New York: Humanities Press.

3:54 Piaget, J. (1930). *The Child's Conception of Physical Causality*, London: Kegan Paul.

3:55 Piaget, J. (1929/1963), *The Child's Conception of the World*, Paterson, N.J.: Littlefield, Adams & Company.

3:56 Piaget, J. (1954). *The Construction of Reality in the Child*, New York: Basic Books.

3:57 Piaget, J. (1945). *La Formation de Symbole Chez l'enfant*, Neuchatel: Delachaux.

3:58 Piaget, J. (1928). *Judgment and Reasoning in the Child*, London: Kegan Paul.

3:59 Piaget, J. (1925/1955). *The Language and Thought of the Child*. International Library of Psychology. (Also Cleveland: The World Publishing Company.)

3:60 Piaget, J. (1932). *The Moral Judgment of the Child*, London: Kegan Paul.

3:61 Piaget, J. (1953). *Origins of Intelligence in Children*, London: Routledge and Kegan Paul.

3:62 Piaget, J. (1951). *Play Dreams, and Imitation in Childhood*, New York: W.W. Norton and Company, Incorporated.

3:63 Piaget, J. (1958). "Principle Factors Determining Intellectual Evaluation from Childhood to Adult Life," in *Outside Readings in Psychology*, E. L. Hartley and R. E. Hartley (eds.), New York: Crowell, pp. 43-55.

3:64 Piaget, J. (1954). "The Problem of Consciousness in Child Psychology: Developmental Changes in Awareness," in *Conference on Problems of Consciousness*, New York: Josiah Macy Foundation, pp. 136-137.

3:65 Preyer, W. (1898). *The Mind of the Child*, (tr. by W.H. Brown), New York: D. Appleton & Co.

3:66 Schium, M.W. (1897). *Notes on the Development of a Child* (in Monograph by D.D. Brown), University of California Studies Berkeley, California: University of Berkeley.

3:67 Sigel, I.E. and F.H. Hooper (1968). *Logical Thinking in Children*, New York, N.Y.: Holt, Rinehart, and Winston, Inc.

3:68 Stern, W. (1914). *Psychologie der Fruhen Kinderheit* (The Psychology of Early Childhood), Leipzig: Quelle & Meyer.

3:69 Sully, J. (1908). *Studies of Childhood*, New York: D. Appleton & Co.

3:70 Tanner, J.M. and B. Inhelder (eds.) (1956). *Discussions on Child Development,* Vol. 1, London: Tavistock Publications, Ltd.

3:71 Wann, K.D. et. al. (1962). *Fostering Intellectual Development in Young Children,* New York: Columbia University.

3:72 Weinberg, N.H. (1959). "Conceptual Level, Self-Centering, and Piaget's Egocentricity," Paper Read at Eastern Psychological Association, Atlantic City.

3:73 Werner, H. (1948). *Comparative Psychology of Mental Development,* Chicago: Follet.

3:74 Werner, H. (1957). "The Concept of Development from a Comparative and Organismic Point of View," in D.B. Harris (ed.), *The Concept of Development: An Issue in the Study of Human Behavior,* Minneapolis: Univ. of Minn. Press.

3:75 Williams, R. (1971/1972). "Testing for Number Readiness: Application of the Piagetian Theory of the Child's Development of the Concept of Number," *The Journal of Educational Research,* 64: 394-6, (May '71).

3:76 Zambrowski, B.B. (1951). *A Study in Childhood Egocentricity as Revealed by Piaget's Tests,* Unpublished Doctoral Dissertation, New School for Social Research.

3:77 Zimiles, H. (1963). "A Note on Piaget's Concept of Conservation," *Child Development,* Vol. 34.

4 Religious Education

4: 1 Acland, R. (1963). *We Teach Them Wrong,* London: Gollancz.

4: 2 Alves, C. (1968). "The Overall Significance of Ronald Goldmann for Religious Education," *Religious Education,* Vol. 63, No. 6, Nov.-Dec.

4: 3 Beirnaert, L. (1962). "The Problem of Conditioning in the Church," in *Readings in European Catechetics,* A. Godin (ed.), Brussels: Lumen Vitae, pp. 63-72.

4: 4 Beiswanger, G.W. (1930). "The Character Value of the Old Testament Stories," *University of Iowa Studies in Character,* Vol. 3, No. 3.

4: 5 Bradford, A. (1961). *Working with Primaries Through the Sunday School,* Nashville, Tenn.: Convention Press.

4: 6 Brown, J.P. (1970). *The Storyteller in Religious Education,* United Church.

4: 7 Brownfield, R. (1973). *First Things,* Dayton, Oh.: Pflaum.

4: 8 Brownfield, R. (ed.), (1974). *Teaching Religion,* Dayton, Oh.: Pflaum.

4: 9 Brusselmans, C. (1970). "Religion for Little Children," Huntington, Ind.: *Our Sunday Visitor.*

4:10 Canaday, J. (1961). "Lessons of the Very Young Masters," *New York Times Magazine,* 28-29, 92-94, August 27.

4:11 Cliff, P.B. (1968). "The Significance of Goldman for Curriculum Materials," *Religious Education,* Vol. 63, No. 6 (Nov.-Dec.).

4:12 Cliff, P.B. and F.M. Cliff (1967). *A Diary for Teachers of Infants,* London: Rupert Hart-Davis.

4:13 Cook, M. (1960). *Bible Teaching for Fours and Fives,* Nashville, Tenn.: Convention Press.

4:14 Cook, S.W. (1962). Editor, *Research Plans Formulated at The Research Planning Workshop on Religious and Character Education,* Mimeographed Report, New York: Religious Education Association.

4:15 Coupez, A. and A. Godin. (1957). "Religious Projective Pictures," *Lumen Vitae Studies in Religious Education,* Vol. 12, No. 2, pp. 200-274.

4:16 Curran, D. (1970). *Who, Me Teach My Child Religion?* Winston Press.

4:17 Finch, S. and E.H. Kreen (1959). "Some Emotional Factors in the Religious Education of Children," *Religious Education,* pp. 36-43.

4:18 Fleming, C.M. (1966). "Research Evidence and Christian Education," *Learning for Living,* Vol. 6, No. 1, (Sept.).

4:19 Franklin, S.P. (1928). "Measurement of the Comprehension Difficulty of the Precepts and Parables of Jesus," *The University of Iowa Studies in Character,* Vol. 2, No. 1.

4:20 Godin, A. (1962). "Importance and Difficulty of Scientific Research in Religious Education: The Problem of Criterion," in *Review of Recent Research Bearing on Religious and Character Formation,* S. W. Cook (ed.), New York: Religious Education Association, pp. 166-174.

4:21 Godin, A. (1955). "Isaac at the Stake," a Psychological Inquiry into the Manner of Presenting a Biblical Episode to Children," in *Lumen Vitae Studies in Religious Education,* Vol. 10, No. 1, pp. 65-92.

4:22 Goldman, R.J. et. al. (1968). *An Analytic Review of the Seabury*

Series and the Church's Teaching. Preschool Through Senior
   High, New York: Executive Council of the Episcopal Church
   in the United States, Department of Education.

4:23 Goldman, R.J. (1966). "The Reform of Religious and Moral Education," Learning for Living, May.

4:24 Greeley, A.M. & P.H. Rossi (1966). The Education of Catholic
   Americans, Chicago: Aldine.

4:25 Hartshorne, H. (1933). Standards & Trends in Religious Education, London: Oxford University Press.

4:26 Hartshorne, H. (1913). Worship in the Sunday School, New
   York: Columbia University Press.

4:27 Hawes, G.K. (1965). "(Mis) Leading Questions," Learning for
   Living, Vol. 4, No. 4.

4:28 Hebron, M.E. (1957). "The Research into the Teaching of Religious Knowledge," Studies in Education, University of Hull.

4:29 Hodgson, G. (1906). Primitive Christian Education, Edinburgh,
   Scotland.

4:30 Howkins, K.G. (1966). Religious Thinking and Religious Education, London: Tyndale Press. (Also see Education, Oxford:
   The Religious Education Press, 1966.)

4:31 Hyde, K.E. et. al. (1956). Sunday Schools Today, Free Church
   Federal Council.

4:32 Lariviere, J.J. (1964). "Religious Knowledge Among Pupils of
   Secular and Religious Catechists," in From Religious Experi-
   ence to a Religious Attitude, A. Godin (ed.), Brussels: Lumen
   Vitae Press, pp. 137-154.

4:33 Lawrence, P.J. (1971). "Secular Christianity and the Education
   of the Person," Study Paper, Theology Seminar, Victoria:
   University of Wellington.

4:34 Lee, J.M. (1975). The Flow of Religious Instruction: A Social
   Science Approach, Mishawaka, Ind.: Religious Education
   Press.

4:35 Lee, J.M. and P. Rooney. (1969). Toward a Future for Religious
   Education, Dayton, Oh.: Pflaum.

4:36 Little, S. (1961). The Role of the Bible in Contemporary Christian Education, John Knox.

4:37 Madge, V. (1971). Introducing Young Children to Jesus, More-
   house-Barlow Press.

4:38 Mathews, H.F. (1966). Revolution in Religious Education, Oxford:
   The Religious Education Press.

4:39 Merlaud, A. (1966). "Family Realities and Education in the Faith,"
        Lumen Vitae Studies in Religious Education, 21, pp. 169-171.
4:40 Newland, M.R. (1967). *The Family and the Bible*, New York:
        Random House.
4:41 Newland, M.R. (1967). "Summer Vacation Bible School," *Living
        Light*, Vol. 4, No. 1, Spring.
4:42 Peatling, J.H. (1968). ed. *An Analytic Review of the Seabury
        Series and The Church's Teaching — Preschool Through
        Senior High*. New York: Executive Council of the Episco-
        pal Church in the United States.
4:43 Pesch, C. (1962). "The Use of Pictures in Catechesis: Present
        Situation and Lasting Problems," in *Lumen Vitae Studies in
        Religious Education*, Vol. 17, pp. 163-172.
4:44 Reichert, R. (1974). *A Learning Process for Religious Education*,
        Dayton, Oh.: Pflaum Publishing.
4:45 Smither, E. (1944). *Primary Children Learn at Church*, New York:
        Abingdon.
4:46 Spilka, B., J. Addison and M. Rosensohn. (1973). "Parents, Self
        and Faith: a Test of Competing Theories of Individual Reli-
        gion Relationships (or is it God and Father, or Mother, or
        Me?"), Paper presented at a meeting of the Society for the
        Scientific Study of Religion, October 26.
4:47 Starbuck, E.D. (1962). *Religious Education in the New World
        View*, in "Religious Education Series," No. 2, Boston:
        American International Association.
4:48 Torrance, E.P. (1963). "The Learning Process in Religious Educa-
        tion," Study Paper prepared for Education Division, Sunday
        School Board of the Southern Baptist Convention.
4:49 Watson, G.B. (1927). *The Scientific Method of Religious Educa-
        tion*, New York: Association Press.
4:50 Wright, K.S. (1974). *Let the Children Paint-Art in Religious Edu-
        cation*, Seabury.
4:51 Young, H. (1962). *Sunday School Work With Fours and Fives*,
        Nashville, Tenn.: Convention Press.

5   Children's Religious Thought & Development

5: 1 Ainsworth, D. (1961). *The Parables: A Study of Some Aspects of
        the Growth of Religious Understanding of Children Aged*

Between 5 and 11 Years, Unpublished Diploma of Education Dissertation, University of Manchester.

5: 2 Batten, R. (1963). "Symposium on 'Readiness for Religion,'" *Learning for Living,* May.

5: 3 Bose, R.G. (1959). "Religious Concepts of Children," *Religious Education,* 24, 831-837.

5: 4 Bovet, P. (1928). *The Child's Religion,* New York: E.P. Dutton & Co.

5: 5 Bovet, P. (1925/1951). *Le Sentiment Religieux et la Psychologie de l'enfant,* Neuchatel, Switzerland: Delachaux.

5: 6 Bradshaw, J. (1949). *A Psychological Study of the Development of Religious Beliefs Among Children & Young People,* Unpublished M.Sc. Dissertation, University of London.

5: 7 Case, R.T. (1930). "A Study of the Placement in the Curriculum of Selected Teaching of the Old Testament Prophets," *The University of Iowa Studies in Character,* Vol. 2, No. 4.

5: 8 Craddick, R.A. (1961). "Size of Santa Claus Drawings as a Function of Time Before and After Christmas," *Journal of Psychological Studies,* 12, pp. 121-125.

5: 9 Craddick, R.A. (1962). "Size of Witch Drawings as a Function of Time Before and After Hallowe'en," *American Psychologist,* 17, p. 307.

5:10 Debot-Sevrin, M.R. (1968). "An Attempt in Experimental Teaching: The Assimilation of a Parable by Normal and Maladjusted 6-7 Year Old Children," *From Cry to Word,* Brussels: Lumen Vitae Press, pp. 134-158.

5:11 Dennis, W. and B. Mallinger, (1949). "Animism and Related Tendencies in Senescence," *Journal of Gerontology,* 4, pp. 218-221.

5:12 Elkind, D. (1961). "The Child's Conception of His Religious Denomination, I: The Jewish Child," *Journal of Genetic Psychology,* 99, pp. 209-225.

5:13 Elkind, D. (1962). "The Child's Conception of His Religious Denomination, II: The Catholic Child," *The Journal of Genetic Psychology,* 101, pp. 185-193.

5:14 Elkind, D. (1963). "The Child's Conception of His Religious Denomination III: The Protestant Child," *Journal of Genetic Psychology,* 103, pp. 291-304.

5:15 Elkind, D., B. Spilka, et. al. (1967). "The Child's Conception of Prayer," *Journal for the Scientific Study of Religion,* 6, 101-109. (Also in *From Cry to Word,* Brussels: Lumen Vitae

Press, 1968).

5:16 Elkind, D. (1970). "The Origins of Religion in the Child," *Review of Religious Research*, Fall, 12, pp. 35-42.

5:17 Elkind, D. and S.F. Elkind (1962). "Varieties of Religious Experience in Young Adolescents," *Journal for the Scientific Study of Religion*, Vol. 2, pp. 103-111.

5:18 Gleason, J.J., Jr. (1974). *Growing Up to God: Eight Steps in Religious Development*, New York: Abingdon.

5:19 Godin, A. (1968). "Genetic Development of the Symbolic Function: The Meaning and Limits of the Works of R. Goldman," *Religious Education*, Vol. 63, No. 6, (Nov.-Dec.).

5:20 Godin, A. (1968). "The Prayers of Petition," editor's preface, *From Cry to Word*, Brussels: Lumen Vitae Press, pp. 13-25.

5:21 Godin, A. (1958). "Psychological Growth and Christian Prayer," *Lumen Vitae Studies in Religious Education*, 13, pp. 517-532.

5:22 Godin, A. and M. Halley. (1971). "Some Developmental Tasks in Christian Education," in *Research on Religious Development*, M. Strommen (ed.), New York: Hawthorne, pp. 109-154.

5:23 Goldman, R.J. (1963). "The Development of Religious Thinking," in *Readiness for Religion*, London: S.L.M. Press, pp. 1-4.

5:24 Goldman, R.J. and E.P. Torrance (1975). "The Meaning and Relevance of Learning Readiness for Curriculum Building in Christian Education," *Character Potential: A Record of Research*, Vol. 7, No. 3, (August), pp. 118-142.

5:25 Goldman, R.J. (1965). *Readiness for Religion.* New York: The Seabury Press, (Also London: Routledge and Kegan Paul.)

5:26 Goldman, R.J. (ed.) (1966-8). *Readiness for Religion Series*, London: Rupert Hart-Davis.

5:27 Goldman, R.J. (1964). "Religious Honesty With Children," *Learning for Living*, Vol. 3, No. 5.

5:28 Goldman, R.J. (1964). *Religious Thinking From Childhood to Adolescence.* London: Routledge and Kegan Paul. (Also New York: The Seabury Press.)

5:29 Goldman, R.J. (1962). *Some Aspects of the Development of Religious Thinking in Childhood and Adolescence.* Unpublished Ph.D. Dissertation, Faculty of Arts, the University of Birmingham (U.K.).

5:30 Graebner, O.E. (1964). "Symposium Research in Religious Development, Part One, Child Concepts of God," *Religious Edu-*

cation, Vol. 59, pp. 234-241.

5:31   Harms, E. (1944). "The Development of Religious Experience in Children," *American Journal of Sociology*, Vol. 50, No. 2, pp. 112-122.

5:32   Hightower, P.R. (1930). "Biblical Information in Relation to Character and Conduct," in *University of Iowa Studies in Character*, Vol. 3, No. 2.

5:33   Hilliard, F.H. (1965). "Children's Religious Thinking," *Learning for Living*, Vol. 5, No. 2.

5:34   Hilliard, F.H. (1963). "Symposium on 'Readiness for Religion,'" in *Learning for Living*, May.

5:35   Hunter, E.F. (1956). *The Questioning Child and Religion*, Boston: Beacon Press.

5:36   Hyde, K.E. (1969). "A Critique of Goldman's Research," *Religious Education*, Vol. 63, No. 6, (Nov.-Dec.), pp. 429-435.

5:37   Hyde, K.E. (1961). "The Religious Concepts of Adolescents," *Religious Education*, pp. 329-334.

5:38   Hyde, K.E. (1965). *Religious Learning in Adolescence*, Educational Monographs v.i.i., University of Birmingham Institute of Education, Edinburgh: Oliver & Boyd.

5:39   Jahoda, G. (1958). "Child Animism: A Critical Survey of Cross-Cultural Research," *Journal of Social Psychology*, 47, pp. 197-212.

5:40   Johnson, J.E. (1961). "An Enquiry into Some of the Religious Ideas of 6-Year-Old Children," Unpublished Thesis, University of Birmingham (U.K.).

5:41   Kligensmith, S.W. (1953). "Child Animism: What the Child Means by 'Alive.'" *Child Development*, 24, pp. 51-61.

5:42   Klingberg, G. (1957). "The Distinction Between Living and Not Living Among 7-10-Year-Old Children, With Some Remarks Concerning the So-Called Animism Controversy," *Journal of Genetic Psychology*, 90, pp. 227-238.

5:43   Klingberg, G. (1959). "A Study of Religious Experience in Children from 9 to 13 Years of Age," *Religious Education*, pp. 211-216.

5:44   Koppe, W.A. (1973). *How Persons Grow in Christian Community*. Philadelphia, Pa.: Fortress.

5:45   Kuhlen, R.G. and M. Arnold. (1944). "Age Differences in Religious Beliefs and Problems During Adolescence," *Journal of Genetic Psychology*, 65, 291-300.

5:46   Lawrence, P.J. (1965). "Children's Thinking About Religion:
        A Study of Concrete Operational Thinking," *Religious Edu
        cation*, pp. 111-116.

5:47   Lee, R.S. (1963). *Your Growing Child and Religion*, London:
        Macmillan.

5:48   Lewis, E. (1956). "The Development of the Religious Attitude in
        Children," in *Christian Essays in Psychiatry*, P. Mairet (ed.),
        London: S.C.M. Press, pp. 83-108.

5:49   Loomba, M. (1944). "The Religious Development of Children,"
        Psychology Abstracts, 345, p. 35.

5:50   Lubin, A.J. (1959). "A Boy's View of Jesus," *The Psychoana-
        lytic Study of the Child*, 14, pp. 155-168.

5:51   Lubin, A.J. (1958). "A Feminine Moses: A Bridge Between Child-
        hood Identifications and Adult Identity," *The International
        Journal of Psychoanalysis*, Vol. 39, pp. 1-12.

5:52   McCann, R.C. (1955). "Developmental Factors in the Growth of
        a Mature Faith," *Religious Education*, 50, pp. 147-155.

5:53   Montessori, M. (1965). *The Child in the Church*, St. Paul: Cate-
        chetical Guild.

5:54   Nelson, C.E. (1967). *Where Faith Begins*, Richmond, Virginia:
        John Knox Press.

5:55   Nelson, M.O. and E.M. Jones (1961). "The Religious Concepts
        in Their Relation to Parental Images," *Adult & Child Before
        God*, Brussels: Lumen Vitae, pp. 105-110.

5:56   O'Neil, R.P. and M. Donovan. (1970). *Children, Church and God*,
        New York: Corpus.

5:57   Patiffe, L. (1965). "A Religious Attitude Scale for Children of
        10-13 Years," in *Child and Adult Before God*, A. Godin (ed.),
        Chicago: Loyola, pp. 87-106.

5:58   Peatling, J.H. (1974). "Cognitive Development in Pupils in
        Grades Four Through Twelve: The Incidence of Concrete
        and Abstract Religious Thinking in American Children,"
        Character Potential: A Record of Research, Vol. 7, No. 1,
        October, pp. 52-61.

5:59   Peatling, J.H. (1968). "The Impact of the Work of Ronald Gold-
        man: A Prospect," *Religious Education*, Vol. 63, No. 6,
        (Nov.-Dec.).

5:60   Peatling, J.H. (1973). *The Incidence of Concrete and Abstract
        Religious Thinking in the Interpretation of Three Bible
        Stories by Pupils Enrolled in Grades Four Through Twelve*

in *Selected Schools in the Episcopal Church in the United States of America,* Ph.D. Dissertation, New York University.

5:61 Reik, T. (1955). "From Spell to Prayer," *Psychoanalysis,* Vol. 3, No. 4, pp. 3-26.

5:62 Robinson, R. (1963). "Honest to Children," in *The Honest to God Debate,* by J.A.T. Robinson. London: S.C.M. Press, Appendix II, pp. 279-287.

5:63 Roloff, E. (1921). "Vom Religiosen Leben der Kinder," *Archiv Fuer Religious Psychologie* (Tubingen), Vol. 2, No. 3, pp. 190-203.

5:64 Ross, M.G. (1950). *Religious Beliefs of Youth,* New York: Association Press.

5:65 Ryan, M.P. (1968). "Dr. Goldman and American Catholic Education," *Religious Education,* Vol. 63, No. 6 (Nov.-Dec.).

5:66 Salman, H.D. (1965). "Summary and Critique of Goldman's Research," *Revue des Sciences Philosophiques et Theologiques,* October, p. 699.

5:67 Schurmans, J. (1955). *Sonte Mentale et Formation Religieuse,* Bruxelles: Association Cath. d'Hygiene Mentale.

5:68 Simmons, A.J. and A.E. Goss. (1957). "Animistic Responses as a Function of Sentence Contexts and Instructions," *Journal of Genetic Psychology,* 91, pp. 181-189.

5:69 Smith, J.J. (1941). "Religious Development in Children," in *Child Psychology,* Skinner and Harriman, New York: Macmillan Co.

5:70 Smith, J.W.D. (1953). *Psychology and Religion in Early Childhood,* London: S.C.M. Press.

5:71 Strauss, A.L. (1951). "The Animism Controversy: Re-Examination of Huang-Lee Donta," *Journal of Genetic Psychology,* 78, 105-113.

5:72 Strommen, M.P. (1963). *Profiles of Church Youth,* St. Louis: Concordia Publishing House.

5:73 Strommen, M.P. (1971). *Research on Religious Development,* New York: Hawthorne Books.

5:74 Van Bunnen, C. (1964). "The Burning Bush: The Symbolic Interpretations Among Children From 5 to 12 Years," in *From Religious Experience to a Religious Attitude,* Brussels: Lumen Vitae Press, pp. 183-194.

5:75 Voeks, V. (1954). "Sources of Apparent Animism in Studies," *Scientific Monthly,* 79, pp. 406-407.

5:76 Wright, D.S. (1962). "A Study of Religious Beliefs in Sixth Form Boys," *University of Leeds Researchers and Studies.*

5:77 Wright, H.D. and W.A. Koppe. (1964). "Children's Potential Religious Concepts," *Character Potential: A Record of Research,* Vol. 2.

5:78 Yeaxlee, B. (1939). *Religion and the Growing Mind,* London: Nisbet.

6 Symbols, Signs, and Religious Imagery

6: 1 Bartlett, F.C. (1921). "The Function of Images," *British Journal of Psychology,* Vol. 11, 320-337.

6: 2 Berefelt, G. (1969). "On Symbol and Allegory," *Journal of Aesthetics and Art Criticism,* 28, pp. 201-213.

6: 3 Bevan, E. (1938). *Symbolism and Belief,* London: Allen and Unwin.

6: 4 Boulding, K.E. (1956). *The Image: Knowledge in Life and Society,* Ann Arbor: University of Michigan Press.

6: 5 Brain, R. (1960). "Symbol and Image," *The Listener,* Vol. 64.

6: 6 Colm, H. (1957). "Religion Symbolism in Child Analysis," *Psychoanalysis,* 2 (1), pp. 39-56.

6: 7 Daves, M. (1967). *Young Reader's Book of Christian Symbolism,* New York: Abingdon.

6: 8 DeValensart, G. (1968). "Modern Religious Pictures: Spontaneous Choices and Understanding of Symbols Among Children Five to Twelve Years," in *From Cry to Word,* A. Godin (ed.), Brussels: Lumen Vitae Press, pp. 119-134.

6: 9 Elaide, M. (1952). *Images and Symbols,* Paris: Gallimard.

6:10 Godin, A., and A. Coupez. (1957). "Religious Projective Pictures," in *Research in Religious Psychology,* Brussels: Lumen Vitae Press.

6:11 Godin, A. (1965). "The Symbolic Function," in *Teaching the Sacraments and Morality,* Chicago: Loyola University Press, pp. 107-120. (Also in *Lumen Vitae Studies in Religious Education,* Vol. 10, No. 2, pp. 277-290, 1955).

6:12 Jung, C.G. (1950). *Creative Forms of the Unconscious,* Zurich: Rascher & Cie.

6:13 Jung, C.G. (1964). *Man and His Symbols,* New York: Dell Press (Laurel ed., 1968).

6:14   Kemp, C.G. (1962). "A Study of Religious Symbolism in Relation
         to Open-Closed Belief Systems," in *Research Plans in the
         Fields of Religion, Values, and Morality*, New York: Reli-
         gious Education Association, pp. 133-141.

6:15   Koch, R. (1930). *The Book of Signs*, New York: Dover Publica-
         tions.

6:16   Krout, J. (1950). "Symbol Elaboration Test S.E.T.: the Relia-
         bility and Validity of a New Projective Technique," *Psycho-
         logical Monograph*, Vol. 64, No. 4.

6:17   Luquet, G.H. (1927). "Le Realisme Intellectuel dans l'art Primi-
         tif: I. Figuration de l'invisible (Intellectual Realism in
         Primitive Art. I. Representation of the Invisible)," *Journal
         de Psychologie Normale et Pathologique*, Vol. 24.

6:18   Markey, J.F. (1928). *The Symbolic Process*, London: Kegan
         Paul, Trench, Trubner.

6:19   Morris, C. (1949). "Signs, Language and Behavior," *Art Bulletin*,
         31, p. 70ff.

6:20   Scholl, S.L. (1965). "Symbols in Religion," *Response in Worship,
         Music; the Arts*, Vol. 6, No. 3, pp. 125-133.

6:21   Whitehead, A.N. (1928). *Symbolism, Its Meaning and Effect*,
         Cambridge: Cambridge University Press.

6:22   Whittemore, C.E. (1974). ed. *Symbols of the Church*, New York:
         Abingdon.

7   Children's Art & Draw-a-"something" tests

7: 1   Alschuler, R.H. and L.B. Hattwich. (1969). *Painting and Person-
         ality: A Study of Young Children*, Chicago: University of
         Chicago Press.

7: 2   "America's Child Artists," (1935). *Literary Digest*, 120: 22,
         (November 16).

7: 3   Armentrout, J.A. (1971). "Effects of Perceptual Training of
         Children's Human Figure Drawing," *Journal of Genetic Psy-
         chology*, 119, (Dec.), pp. 281-287.

7: 4   Ballard, P.B. (1913). "What Children Like to Draw," *Journal of
         Experimental Pedagogy*, Vol. 2, pp. 127-129.

7: 5   Barnes, E. (1891). "Notes on Children's Drawings," *Pedagogical
         Seminary*, Vol. 1, pp. 445-447.

7: 6   Barnes, E. (1893). "A Study of Children's Drawings," *Pedagogical*

Seminary, Vol. 2, pp. 451-463.

7: 7 Battist, S. (1967). "Child Art and Visual Perception," *Art Education,* Vol. 20, No. 1, pp. 20-27.

7: 8 "The Bewildering Art of Children," (1922). *Literary Digest,* Vol. 34, No. 35, (July 1).

7: 9 Biddle, G. (1934). "Creative Art in Children," *American Magazine of Art,* 27, pp. 532-36.

7:10 Bried, C. (1950). "Le Dessin de L'Enfort; Premieres Representations Humaines," ("The Child's Drawings; First Human Representations"). *Enfrance,* 3, pp. 261-275.

7:11 Brown, D.D. (1897). "Notes on Children's Drawings," *University of California Publications,* Berkeley, Ca.: University of California.

7:12 "Child Artists of Paris," (1918). *Literary Digest,* Vol. 28, (August 17).

7:13 Claparide, E. (1907). "Plan d'Experiences Collectives Sue le Dessin des Enfants," *Archives de Psychologie,* Vol. 6, pp. 276-278.

7:14 Clark, A.B. (1902). "The Child's Attitude Toward Perspective Problems," in *Studies in Education* by Barnes, E., Stanford, Ca.: Stanford University Press, Vol. 1, pp. 283-294.

7:15 Clark, J.S. (1897). "Some Observations on Children's Drawing," *Educational Review,* January, 13, pp. 76-82.

7:16 Clark, K.B. and M.P. Clark. (1952). "Racial Identification and Preference in Negro Children," *Readings in Social Psychology,* Newcomb and Hartley (eds.), New York: Holt.

7:17 Cook, E. (1885). "Art Teaching & Child Nature," *London Journal of Education.*

7:18 Coyle, F.A., Jr. and R. Eisenman. (1969). "Santa Claus Drawings by Negro and White Children," *Journal of Social Psychology,* 80, pp. 201-205.

7:19 Dennis, W. (1966). *Group Values Through Children's Drawings,* New York: John Wiley and Sons.

7:20 Dennis, W. (1957). "Performance of Near Eastern Children on the Draw-a-Man Test," *Child Development,* Vol. 28, No. 4, pp. 427-430.

7:21 Dennis, W. (1963). "Value Expressed in Children's Drawings," in *Readings in Child Psychology,* W. Dennis (ed.), Englewood Cliffs, N.J.: Prentice-Hall.

7:22 Dunn, M.B. (1954). *Global Evaluation of Children's Drawings of*

"Person" and "Self," Unpublished Doctoral Dissertation, Columbia University.

7:23 Elkisch, P. (1945). "Children's Drawings in a Projective Technique," *Psychological Monograph,* 58, No. 1.

7:24 Eng, H. (1931). *The Psychology of Children's Drawings,* London: Routledge and Kegan Paul.

7:25 Eng, H. (1957). *The Psychology of Child and Youth Drawing,* New York: Humanities Press.

7:26 England, A.O. (1943). "A Psychological Study of Children's Drawings," *American Journal of Orthopsychiatry,* 13, pp. 525-531.

7:27 Eysenck, S.B., T. Russell, and H.J. Eysenck. (1969). "Extra-version, Intelligence, and Ability to Draw a Person," *Perceptual and Motor Skills,* 30, pp. 925-926.

7:28 Fuller, G.B., M. Preuss, and W.F. Hawkins. (1969). "The Validity of the Human Figure Drawings With Disturbed and Normal Children," *Journal of School Psychology,* 8, pp. 54-56.

7:29 Gaitskell, C.D. (1958). *Children and Their Art,* New York: Harcourt, Brace, & Co.

7:30 Gasqrek, K.A. (1951). *A Study of the Consistency and the Reliability of Certain of the Formal and Structural Characteristics of Children's Drawings,* Unpublished Doctoral Dissertation, Columbia University.

7:31 Golomb, C. (1969/1970). "Children's Representation of the Human Figure Syncretism of Invention," *Proceedings of the 77th Annual Convention of the American Psychological Association,* 4, pp. 479-480.

7:32 Golomb, C. (1969). "The Effects of Models, Media, and Instructions on Children's Representation of the Human Figure," *Dissertation Abstracts International,* 30, pp. 1884-5.

7:33 Goodenough, F.L. (1931). "Children's Drawings," in *A Handbook of Child Psychology,* C. Murchison (ed.), Worcester, Mass.: Clark University Press.

7:34 Goodenough, F. (1926). *Measurement of Intelligence by Drawings,* New York: Harcourt Brace and World.

7:35 Goodenough, F.L. (1928). "Studies in the Psychology of Children's Drawings," *Psychological Bulletin,* 25, pp. 272-283.

7:36 Goodenough, F. and D.B. Harris. (1950). "Studies in the Psychology of Children's Drawings: II, 1928-1949," *Psychological Bulletin,* 47, pp. 369-433.

7:37 Goodnow, J.J. and S. Friedman. (1971). "Orientation in Children's Human Figure Drawings: An Aspect of Graphic Language," *Developmental Psychology*, 7, (July), pp. 10-16.

7:38 Gotze, K. (1898). *Das Kindes als Kunstler*, Hamburg.

7:39 Graham, S.R. (1956). "A Study of Reliability in Human Figure Drawings," *Journal of Projective Techniques*, 20, pp. 385-386.

7:40 Grossman, M. (1971). "Motor Coordination and Young Children's Drawing Abilities," *Child Study Journal*, 1, (Summer), pp. 213-215.

7:41 Grozinger, W. (1955). *Scribbling, Drawing and Painting*, New York: Praeger.

7:42 Harms, E. (1941). "Child Art as Aid in the Diagnosis of Juvenile Neuroses," *American Journal of Orthopsychiatry*, 11, (April), pp. 191-209.

7:43 Harris, D.B. (1963). *Children's Drawings as Measures of Intellectual Maturity*, New York: Harcourt, Brace & World.

7:44 Harris, D.B. (1950). "Intra-individual vs. Inter-individual Consistency in Children's Drawings of a Man," *American Psychologist*, 5, p. 293.

7:45 Herrick, M.A. (1893). "Children's Drawings," *Pedagogical Seminary*, Vol. 3, pp. 338-339.

7:46 Holtzman, W.H. (1952). "The Examiner as a Variable in the Draw-a-Person Test," *Journal of Consulting & Clinical Psychology*, 16, pp. 145-148.

7:47 Hurlock, E.B. (1934). "Children's Drawings: An Experimental Study of Perception," *Child Development*, Vol. 5, No. 2.

7:48 Kato, M. (1936). "A Genetic Study of Children's Drawings of Man," *Japanese Journal of Experimental Psychology*, 3, pp. 175-185 (Psychol. Abstr., 11:3000).

7:49 Katzaroff, M.D. (1910). "Qu est ce que les Enfants Dessinent?" *Archives de Psychologie*, Vol. 9, p. 125.

7:50 Kellogg, R. (1969). *Analyzing Children's Art*, Palo Alto, Ca.: Mayfield Publishing Co.

7:51 Kellogg, R. (1966). *Child Art: The Beginnings of Self-Affirmation*, H.P. Lewis (ed.), Berkeley: Diablo Press.

7:52 Kellogg, R. and S. O'Dell (1967). *The Psychology of Children's Art*, Delmar, California: CRM Associates for Random House.

7:53 Kellogg, R. (1967). "Understanding Children's Art," *Psychology Today*, Vol. 1, No. 1, pp. 16-25.

7:54 Kellogg, R. (1959). *What Children Scribble and Why*, Palo Alto,

Ca.: National Press.

7:55 Knopf, I.J. and T.W. Richards. (1952). "The Child's Differentiation of Sex as Reflected in Drawings of the Human Figure," *Journal of Genetic Psychology*, 81, pp. 99-112.

7:56 Koestler, A. (1964). *The Age of Creation*, New York: Macmillan.

7:57 Koppitz, E.M. (1969). "Emotional Indicators on Human Figure Drawings of Boys and Girls from Lower and Middle-Class Backgrounds," *Journal of Consulting & Clinical Psychology*, 25, pp. 432-434.

7:58 Korzenik, D. (1973/4). "Role-taking and Children's Drawings," *Studies in Art Education*, Vol. 15, No. 3, pp. 17-24.

7:59 Korzenik, D. (1971). *Visual Definitions: Communication in Children's Drawings,* Unpublished Manuscript, Harvard Graduate School of Education.

7:60 Lark-Horowitz, B. and J. Norton. (1960). "Children's Art Abilities the Interrelations and Factorial Structure of Ten Characteristics," *Child Development*, Vol. 31.

7:61 Lehner, G.F.J. and E.K. Gunderson. (1952). "Reliability of Graphic Indices in a Projective Test (the Draw-A-Person)," *Journal of Consulting and Clinical Psychology*, Vol. 8.

7:62 Lewis, H.P. (1967). "The Art of Childhood Reconsidered," *Art Education*, Vol. 20, No. 9.

7:63 Loney, J. (1971). "The Sun as a Measure of Dependency in Children's Drawings," *Journal of Consulting and Clinical Psychology*, 27, October, pp. 513-514.

7:64 Lowenfeld, V. (1954). *Your Child and His Art*, New York: The Macmillan Co.

7:65 Lukens, H. (1896). "A Study of Children's Drawings in the Early Years," *Pedagogical Seminary*, Vol. 4, pp. 79-110.

7:66 Luguet, G.H. (1912). "Le Premier Age du Dessin Enfantin," *Archives de Psychologie*, Vol. 12, pp. 14-20.

7:67 Luguet, G.H. (1913). *Les Dessins d'un Enfant* (The Drawings of a Child), Paris: F. Alcan.

7:68 Machotka, P. (1966). "Aesthetic Criteria in Childhood: Justification of Preference," *Child Development*, 37, pp.877-885.

7:69 Machover, K. (1953). "Human Figure Drawings of Children," *Journal of Projective Techniques*, Vol. 17.

7:70 Maitland, L. (1895). "What Children Draw to Please Themselves,", *Inland Educator*, Vol. 1, p. 87.

7:71 Marsh, E. (1957). "Paul Klee and the Art of Children," *College Art Journal,* Vol. 15, No. 16, (January), pp. 132-45.

7:72 McBroom, P. (1968). "Mining the Child's Art," *Science News,* Vol. 93, No. 4.

7:73 McCarty, S.A. (1924). *Children's Drawings,* Baltimore: Williams and Wilkins.

7:74 McWhinnie, H.J. (1972). "A Note on Methodology in Using Children's Figure Drawing to Assess Racial and Cultural Differences," *Studies in Art Education,* Vol. 13, No. 2, pp. 30-33.

7:75 Meili-Dworetzki, G. (1957). *Das Bild Des Menchen in der Vorstellung und Darstellung des Kleinkindes* (The Images of Men in the Conception and Representation of Children), Bern: Verlag Hand Huber.

7:76 Mumford, L. (1936). "The Child as Artist," *New Republic,* 47: 165-67, (June).

7:77 Nelson, T.M. and M.E. Hanney (1966). "Drawing Techniques: 6-7 Year-Olds," *Studies in Art Education,* Vol. 8, No. 2, p. 58.

7:78 O'Shea, M.V. (1894). "Children's Expression Through Drawing," Proceedings of the National Education Assoc., p. 1015.

7:79 Partridge, L. (1902). "Children's Drawings of Men & Women," in *Studies in Education,* E. Barnes (ed.), Stanford, Ca.: Stanford University Press, Vol. 2, pp. 163-179.

7:80 Perez, M.B. (1888). *L'Art et la Poesie chez l'Enfant,* Paris.

7:81 Porter, K.A. (1927). "Children and Art," *Nation,* 124: 23-34, (March 2).

7:82 Prowller, W. (1973). "The Role of the Body in Early Artistic Expression," *Art Education,* Vol. 26, No. 3, pp. 11-15.

7:83 Prudhommeau, M. (1947). *Le Dessin de l'Enfant* (The Child's Drawing), Paris: Presses Univer. de France.

7:84 Rabello, S. (1932). "Characteristics do desenho Infantil, (Characteristics of Children's Drawings)," *Boletin Deretoria Tecn. de Education,* Vol. 2.

7:85 Rey, A. (1946). "Epreuves de Dessin Temoins du Developpment Mental: I (The Use of Drawings as Measures of Mental Development"). *Archives de Psychologie, Geneva,* Vol. 32.

7:86 Ricci, C. (1894). "L'Arte dei Bambini, Balogna," (Tr. by Maitland in *Pedagogical Seminary,* Vol. 3.

7:87 Rouma, Georges (1913). *Le Langage Graphique de l'Enfant,*

Brussels: Misch and Tron.

7:88 Schnall, M. (1969/1970). "Representations and Reproductions in Children's Drawings and Descriptions of Events," *Proceedings of the 77th Annual Convention of the American Psychological Association*, 4; pp. 481-482.

7:89 Struempger, D.J. (1971). "Validation of Two Quality Scales for Children's Figure Drawings," *Perceptual and Motor Skills*, 32, June, pp. 887-893.

7:90 Tomlinson, R.R. (1942). *Picture Making by Children*, Scranton, Pa.: International Textbook Co.

7:91 Van Der Horst, L. (1950). "Affect, Expression & Symbolic Junction in the Drawing of Children," in *Feelings and Emotions*, M.L. Reymert, ed., New York: McGraw-Hill.

7:92 Vroegh, K. (1969). "Lack of Sex-Role Differentiation in Preschoolers' Figure Drawings," *Journal of Projective Techniques*, 34, pp. 38-40.

8   Artistic Development & Psychology of Art

8: 1 Baker, H. and R. Kellogg. (1967). "A Developmental Study of Children's Drawings," *Pediatrics*, Vol. 40, No. 3.

8: 2 Barnhart, E.N. (1942). "Developmental Stages in Compositional Construction in Children's Drawings," *Journal of Experimental Education*, Vol. 11, pp. 156-184.

8: 3 Bell, J.E. (1952). "Perceptual Development and the Drawings of Children," *American Journal of Orthopsychiatry*, 22, pp. 386-393.

8: 4 Burk, F. (1902). "The Genetic vs. The Logical Order in Drawing," *Pedagogical Seminary*, Vol. 9, pp. 296-323.

8: 5 Dennis, W. and E. Raskin. (1960). "Further Evidence Concerning the Effect of Handwriting Habits Upon the Location of Drawings," *Journal of Consulting and Clinical Psychology*, Vol. 24, No. 6, pp. 548-549.

8: 6 Dennis, W. (1958). "Handwriting Conventions as Determinants of Human Figure Drawings," *Journal of Consulting and Clinical Psychology*, Vol. 22, No. 4, pp. 293-295.

8: 7 Desai, K. (1958). *Developmental Stages in Drawing a Cow*, Unpublished B.A. Thesis, Baroda University.

8: 8 Hildreth, G. (1941). *The Child Mind is Evolution: A Study of*

Developmental Sequence in Drawing, New York: King's
Crown Press.

8: 9 Hogg, J. (ed.) (1970). *Psychology and the Visual Arts,* New York:
Penguin Books, Inc.

8:10 Lewis, H.P. (1962). "Developmental Stages in Children's Representation of Spatial Relations in Drawings," *Studies in Art
Education,* Vol. 3, No. 2, (Spring), pp. 69-76.

8:11 Luquet, G.H. (1929). "L'Evolution du Dessin Enfantin." (The
Development of Childish Drawing), *Bulletin of Social Binet,*
Vol. 29.

8:12 McFee, J.K. (1970). *Preparation for Art,* Belmont, California:
Wadsworth.

8:13 Meier, N.C. (ed.) (1929). "Studies in the Psychology of Art,"
Vol. III in *Psychological Monographs,* Vol. 51, No. 5.

8:14 Rogolsky, M.M. (1967). "Artistic Creativity and Adaptive Regres-
sion in Third-Grade Children," *Journal of Projective Techniques,* 32, No. 1, 53-62.

8:15 Schaeffer-Simmern, F. (1948). *The Unfolding of Artistic Activity,*
Berkeley & Los Angeles: University of California Press.

9   Religious Denominations & Their Belief Systems

9: 1 Argow, W. (1970). *Unitarian Universalism: Some Questions
Answered,* (pamphlet), Boston, Massachusetts: Unitarian
Universalist Association.

9: 2 Bartlett, I.H. (ed.) (1957). *Channing: Unitarian Christianity and
Other Essays,* New York: Bobbs-Merrill Company, Inc.

9: 3 Booth, J.N. (1970). *Introducing Unitarian Universalism* (pamphlet), Boston, Massachusetts: Unitarian Universalist Ass'n.

9: 4 Brewer, E.D.C. (1974). "Exploring Religions," in *Character
Potential: A Record of Research,* Vol. 6, No. 4.

9: 5 Donin, Rabbi H.H. (1972). *To Be A Jew,* New York, N.Y.:
Basic Books.

9: 6 Glazer, N. (1974). *American Judaism,* Chicago: University of
Chicago Press.

9: 7 Harmon, N.B. (1974). *Understanding The United Methodist
Church,* New York: Abingdon.

9: 8 Hordurn, W.E. (1968). *A Layman's Guide to Protestant Theology,* New York: Macmillan.

9: 9 James, W. (1902). *Varieties of Religious Experience*, New York: Longmans.

9:10 Marshall, G.N. (1970). *Unitarians and Universalists Believe* (pamphlet), Boston, Massachusetts: Unitarian Universalist Ass'n.

9:11 Mikelson, T. (1975). "Extended Family" (Sermon), The Unitarian-Universalist Society of Iowa City, Iowa, October 5, 1975.

9:12 Rosten, L., (ed.). (1975). *Religions of America*, New York, N.Y.: Simon and Schuster.

9:13 Schaller, L.E. (1975). *Hey, That's Our Church*, New York: Abingdon Press.

9:14 Steinberg, M. (1947). *Basic Judaism*, New York, N.Y.: Harcourt, Brace & World.

9:15 Whalen, W.J, (1967). *The Unitarian Universalists,* (pamphlet), Chicago, Illinois: Claretian Publications.

9:16 *What Makes Us Different?* (pamphlet, 1962), Boston, Massachusetts: Unitarian Universalist Association.

9:17 Williams, C.W. (1972). *John Wesley's Theology Today,* New York: Abingdon.

9:18 Williams, J.P. (1969). *What Americans Believe and How They Worship,* New York, N.Y.: Harper & Row.

10   Aesthetics, Art Criticism, & Philosophy

10: 1 Alexander, C.W. (1964). *Notes on the Synthesis of Form,* Cambridge, Ma.: Harvard University Press.

10: 2 Arnheim, R. (1954). *Art and Visual Perception,* Berkeley: University of California Press.

10: 3 Arnheim, R. (1969). *Visual Thinking,* Berkeley and Los Angeles: University of California Press.

10: 4 Ayer, F.C. (1916). *The Psychology of Drawing.* Baltimore: Warwick & York, Inc.

10: 5 Cohen, J. (1920). "The Use of Objective Criteria in the Measurement of Drawing Ability," *Pedagogical Seminary,* Vol. 27, pp. 137-151.

10: 6 Denman, W.G. (1962). *Art and Social Order,* New York: Dover Publications.

10: 7 Ehrenzweig, A. (1967). *The Hidden Order of Art,* Berkeley and Los Angeles: University of California Press.

10: 8 Ehrenzweig, A. (1965). *The Psychoanalysis of Artistic Vision and*

Hearing: An Introduction to a Theory of Unconscious Perception, New York: Braziller Press.

10: 9   Eisenman, R. (1967). "Birth Order and Sex Differences in Aesthetic Preference for Complexity-Simplicity," *Journal of General Psychology,* 77, pp. 121-126.

10:10   Eisenman, R. and N.R. Schussel. (1969). "Creativity, Birth Order, and Preference for Symmetry," *Journal of Consulting and Clinical Psychology,* 34, pp. 275-280.

10:11   Feldman, E.B. (1970). *Becoming Human Through Art: Aesthetic Experience in the School,* Englewood Cliffs, N.J.: Prentice-Hall.

10:12   Fisher, S. and R. Fisher. (1950). "Test of Certain Assumptions Regarding Figure Drawing Analysis," *Journal of Abnormal and Social Psychiatry,* 45, pp. 727-732.

10:13   Flannery, M.E. (1968). "Art Education and the Interplay Between the Intellect and Imagination in Artistic Creation," *Dissertation Abstracts,* 29, p. 833.

10:14   Fry, R. (1920). *Vision and Design,* London: Chatto and Windus.

10:15   Gibson, J.J. (1950). *The Perception of the Visual World,* Greenwood Press.

10:16   Gibson, E. (1957). *Painting and Reality,* New York: Bolligen Series XXXV, Pantheon Books.

10:17   Gombrich, E.H. (1960). *Art and Illusion,* New York: Pantheon Books.

10:18   Gombrich, E.H. (1963). *Meditations on a Hobby Horse and Other Essays on the Theory of Art.* London: Phiadon.

10:19   Goodman, N. (1968). *Languages of Art, An Approach to a Theory of Symbols,* Indianapolis: Bobbs-Merrill, ch. 1 and 6.

10:20   Granit, A.R. (1921). "A Study of the Perception of Form," *British Journal of Psychology,* Vol. 12, pp. 223-252.

10:21   Harris, N.G.E. (1963). "Goodman's Account of Representation," *Journal of Aesthetics and Art Criticism,* 31, pp. 323-329.

10:22   Kaufman, I. (1966). *Art and Education in Contemporary Culture,* New York: The Macmillan Co.

10:23   Keel, J.S. (1972). "The Roots of Aesthetic Experience," *Art Education,* Vol. 25, No. 3, pp. 4-8.

10:24   Kris, E. (1952). *Psychoanalytic Explorations in Art,* New York: International University Press.

10:25 Lipman, M. (1956/7). "The Aesthetic Presence of the Body,"
        Journal of Aesthetics and Art Criticism, Vol. 15, pp.
        415-424.
10:26 Lowenfeld, V. (1957). *Creative and Mental Growth* (third
        Edition). New York: Macmillan Company.
10:27 Lowenfeld, V. (1939). *The Nature of Creative Activity*, New
        York: Harcourt, Brace and Company, p. 272.
10:28 Manns, J.W. (1971). "Representation, Relativism and Resem-
        blance," *British Journal of Aesthetics*, Vol. 11, No. 3,
        pp. 281-288.
10:29 Peltz, R. (1972). "Nelson Goodman on Picturing, Describing,
        and Exemplifying," *The Journal of Aesthetic Education*,
        Vol. 6, No. 3, pp. 71-86.
10:30 Pole, D. (1974). "Goodman and the 'Naive View' of Repre-
        sentation," *British Journal of Aesthetics*, Vol. 14, No. 1,
        pp. 68-81.
10:31 Read, H. (1945). *Education Through Art*, London: Faber and
        Faber, p. 320.
10:32 Richardson, J.A. (1968). "Modern Theology and Aesthetic Edu-
        cation," *The Journal of Aesthetic Education*, Vol. 2, No.
        2, pp. 67-78.
10:33 Savile, A. (1971). "Nelson Goodman's 'Language of Art': A
        Study," *British Journal of Aesthetics*, 11, No. 1, pp. 3-28.
10:34 Smith, C.M. (1969). "Symbolic Systems, Cognitive Efficacy,
        and Aesthetic Education," *The Journal of Aesthetic Edu-
        cation*, Vol. 3, No. 4, pp. 123-136.
10:35 Weitz, M. (1971). "Professor Goodman on the Aesthetic,"
        Journal of Aesthetics and Art Criticism, 29, pp. 485-489.

11   Sociology, Psychology, & Philosophy of Religion

11: 1 Alconer, L. (1962). "Clinical Interpretation of the Religious
        Behavior," in *Colpa e Colpenvolezza*, Milan: Vita e Pen-
        siero, pp. 73-89.
11: 2 Allport, G.W. (1960). *The Individual and His Religion*, New
        York: Macmillan.
11: 3 Ames, E. (1910). *Psychology of Religious Experience*, Boston:
        Houghton-Mifflin Company.
11: 4 Argyle, M. (1958). *Religious Behavior*, London: Routledge.

11: 5 Barbour, I.G. (1974). *Myth, Models, & Paradigms — A Comparative Study in Science & Religion*, Harper & Row.

11: 6 Brown, L.B. (1966). "Egocentric Thought in Petitionary Prayer: A Cross-Cultural Study," *Journal of Social Psychology, 68*, pp. 197-210.

11: 7 Brown, L.B. (1968). "Some Attitudes Underlying Petitionary Prayer," in *From Cry to Word*, A. Godin (ed.), Brussels: Lumen Vitae Press, pp. 65-84.

11: 8 Brown, L.B. (1962). "A Study of Religious Belief," *British Journal of Psychology*, Vol. 53.

11: 9 Buber, M. (1923). *I and Thou*, Leipzig: Insel-Verlag, (translated by R. Gregor, 1937, Edinburgh: Clark Press).

11:10 Clark, E.T. (1929). *The Psychology of Religious Awakening*, New York.

11:11 Clark, W.H. (1958). *The Psychology of Religion*, New York: Macmillan.

11:12 Conklin, E.S. (1929). *Psychology of Religious Adjustment*, New York: Macmillan Company.

11:13 Deconchy, J.P. (1967). "Une tentative d'epistemolgie de la Pensee Religieuse," *Archives de Sociologie des Religions*, Vol. 24, (Juillet), pp. 141-145.

11:14 Draper, E., G.G. Meyer, A. Parzen, and G. Samuelson. (1965). "On the Diagnostic Value of Religious Ideation: *Archives of General Psychiatry*, September, 13, pp. 202-207, Reprinted in *Insight*, Winter 1966, pp. 45-49.

11:15 Dresser, H.W. (1929). *Outlines of the Psychology of Religion*, New York: T.Y. Crowell Company.

11:16 Dunlap, K. (1946). *Religion: Its Function in Human Life*, New York: McGraw-Hill.

11:17 Elaide, M. (1948). *Traite d'histoire des Religions*. Paris: Payot.

11:18 Farrell, B.A. (1955). "Psychological Theory and the Belief in God," *International Journal of Psychoanalysis, 36*, pp. 187-204.

11:19 Fishbein, M. (1965). "A Consideration of Beliefs, Attitudes and Their Relationships," in *Current Studies in Social Psychology*, I. D. Steiner and M. Fishbein (eds.), New York: Holt, Rinehart, and Winston.

11:20 Forest, A. (1968). "Concerning the Esthetic and Religious Experience," *Humanitas*, 4, pp. 151-160.

11:21 Freud, S. (1938). "Totem and Taboo," in *The Basic Writings of*

Sigmund Freud, New York: Modern Library.

11:22 Fromm, E. (1941). *Escape From Freedom*, New York: Holt, Rhinehart and Winston.

11:23 Fromm, E. (1952). *Psychoanalysis and Religion*, New Haven: Yale University Press.

11:24 Goldman, R.J. (1963). "What is Religious Knowledge?" *National Froebel Foundation Bulletin*, No. 117.

11:25 Gruehn, W. (1926). *Religion-Psychologie*, Breslau: Hut.

11:26 Heiler, F. (1932). *Prayer: A Study in the History & Psychology of Religion*, London: Oxford University Press.

11:27 Hodge, A. (1931). *Prayer and Its Psychology*, New York: Macmillan.

11:28 Hyde, K. E. (1963). "Religious Concepts and Religious Attitudes," *University of Birmingham Review*, February.

11:29 Iisager, H. (1949). "Factors Influencing the Formation and Change of Political and Religious Attitudes," *The Journal of Social Psychology*, 29, pp. 253-65.

11:30 Jones, E. (1944). "The Psychology of Religion," in *Psychoanalysis Today*, S. Lorand (ed.), New York: International University Press.

11:31 Jung, C.G. (1938). *Psychology and Religion*, New Haven: Yale University Press.

11:32 Liege, P.A. (1967). "Religion Which is Not Faith," *Lumen Vitae Studies in Religious Education*, 22, pp. 427-440.

11:33 Oates, W. (1973). *The Psychology of Religion*, Word Press.

11:34 O'Dea, T.F. (1961). "Five Dilemmas in the Institutionalization of Religion," *Journal for the Scientific Study of Religion*, Vol. 1, No. 1, pp. 30-41.

11:35 O'Dea, T.F. (1966). *The Sociology of Religion*, Englewood Cliffs, N.J.: Prentice-Hall.

11:36 Piaget, J. (1923). *La Psychologie et les For Religieuses*, Geneve: Labor.

11:37 Pohier, J.M. (1967). *Psychologie et Theologie*, Paris: Cerf.

11:38 Radke-Yarrow, M. et. al. (1952). "The Role of Parents in the Development of Children's Ethnic Attitudes," *Child Development*, Vol. 23, No. 1.

11:39 Siegman, A.W. (1961). "An Empirical Investigation of the Psychoanalytic Theory of Religious Behavior," *Journal for the Scientific Study of Religion*, 1, pp. 74-78.

11:40 Starbuck, E.D. (1900). *Psychology of Religion*, New York:

Charles Scribner's Sons.

11:41 Strunk, O. (1962). *Religion a Psychological Interpretation*, New York: Abingdon Press.

11:42 Thouless, R.H. (1932). *An Introduction to the Psychology of Religion*, London: Cambridge University Press.

11:43 Vergote, A. (1966). *Psychologie Religieuse*, Brussels: Dessart.

12   Miscellaneous

12: 1 Bannan, J.F. (1967). *The Philosophy of Merlsan-Ponty*, New York: Harcourt, Brace & World, Inc.

12: 2 Barnes, E. (1891). *Studies in Education*, Stanford, Ca.: Stanford University Press, Vol. 1.

12: 3 Bell, J.E. (1948). *Projective Techniques*, New York: Longmans.

12: 4 Bruner, J.S. (1960). *The Process of Education*, Cambridge, Mass.: Harvard University Press.

12: 5 Burt, C. (1921). *Mental and Scholastic Tests*, Report of the London County Council.

12: 6 Chamberlain, A.F. (1900). *The Child: A Study in the Evolution of Man*, New York: Charles Scribner's Sons.

12: 7 Clothier, F. (1938). "The Social Development of the Young Child," *Child Development*, Vol. 9, No. 3.

12: 8 Coles, R. (1967). *Children of Crisis*, Boston: Little and Brown, (Volume I).

12: 9 Coles, R. (1971). *Migrants, Sharecroppers, Mountaineers*, Boston: Little and Brown, (Volume II).

12:10 Coles, R. (1971). *The South Goes North*, Boston: Little and Brown, (Volume III).

12:11 Coopersmith, S. (1967). *The Antecedents of Self-Esteem*, San Francisco: Freeman.

12:12 Cruchen, G. (1969). *The Transformations of Childhood*, Dayton: Pflau, Bassim.

12:13 Dennis, W. (1968). "Racial Change in Negro Drawings," *Journal of Psychology*, Vol. 69, pp. 129-130.

12:14 Dennis, W. and A. Uras. (1965). "The Religious Content of Human Figure Drawings Made by Nuns," *Journal of Psychology*, Vol. 61, pp. 263-266.

12:15 Elaide, M. (1957). *Mythes, Reves et Mysteres*, Paris: Gallimard.

12:16 Fleming, C.M. (1968). "Retrospect," *Bulletin of the Univer-*

sity of London Institute of Education, new series 15.

12:17 Goldstein, K. (1940). *Human Nature in the Light of Psychopathology*, New York: Schocken Books.

12:18 Gould, J. and W. Kolb, eds., (1964). *A Dictionary of the Social Sciences*, New York: N.Y. Free Press of Glencoe.

12:19 Hammer, E. (ed.) (1958). *The Clinical Application of Projective Drawings*, Springfield, Ill.: Charles C. Thomas, Publisher.

12:20 Harms, E. (1930). "Uber eine neue Art und Verwendung von Tests," *Schweiz. Psychologysisch Rdsch.* August-September, Nos. 1 and 2.

12:21 Hellersberg, E.F. (1950). *The Individual's Relation to Reality in Our Culture*, Springfield, Ill.: Charles C. Thomas.

12:22 Huber, R.J. (1975). "Social Interest Revisited: A Second Look at Adler," *Character Potential: A Record of Research*, Vol. 7, No. 2.

12:23 Hunt, J. McV. (1962). *Intelligence and Experience*, New York: Ronald Press.

12:24 Johnson, R.C. (1959). *A Study of Children's Moral Judgments*, Unpublished Doctoral Dissertation, University of Minnesota.

12:25 Kerschensteiner, D.G. (1905). *Die Entwickelung der Zeichnerischen Begabung*, Munich: Gerber.

12:26 Kline, L.W. & G.L. Carey. (1922). "A Measuring Scale for Freehand Drawing," *Johns Hopkins Studies in Education*, No. 5.

12:27 Lawlor, M. (1965). *Out of This World: A Study of Catholic Values*, London: Sheed & Ward.

12:28 Levy, S. (1950). "Figure Drawing as a Projective Test," in *Projective Psychology*, ed. by L.E. Abt and L. Ballak, pp. 257-297.

12:29 Levy-Bruhl, L. (1922). *La Mentalite Primitive*, Paris: Alcan.

12:30 Liu, C.H. (1950). *The Influence of Cultural Background on the Moral Judgment of the Child*, Unpublished Doctoral Dissertation, Colombia University.

12:31 Lobsein, M. (1905). "Kinderzerchnung and Kunstkanon," *Zeitschrift Fuer Pedagogisch Psychologie*, Vol. 7, pp. 393-404.

12:32 Loomis, E.A. Jr. (1960). *Self in Pilgrimage*, New York: Harper and Brothers.

12:33 MacRae, D. (1950). *The Development of Moral Judgment in Children,* Unpublished Doctoral Dissertation, Harvard University.

12:34 Mathews, S. and G. Smith, eds. (1921). *A Dictionary of Religion and Ethics,* New York, N.Y.: Macmillan Company.

12:35 Moran, G. (1965). *Theology of Revelation,* New York: Herder & Herder.

12:36 Murdy, W.H. (1975). "Anthropocentrism: A Modern Version," *Science,* 187, No. 4182, (March 28).

12:37 Nelson, M.O., and E.J. Jones. (1957). "An Application of the Q-technique to the Study of Religious Concepts," *Psychological Reports, 3,* pp. 293-297.

12:38 Nouwen, H.J.M. (1969). *Intimacy,* Notre Dame: Fides, pp.5-20.

12:39 Nunn, C.Z. (1964). "Child Control Through a 'Coalition with God,'" *Child Development,* Vol. 35.

12:40 Osgood, C.E., G.J. Suci and P.H. Tannenbaum (1957). *The Measurement of Meaning,* Urbana, Ill.: University of Illinois Press.

12:41 O'Shea, M.V. (1897). "Some Aspects of Drawing," *Educational Review,* Vol. 14, pp. 263-284.

12:42 Piaget, J. (1931). "Children's Philosophies," in *Handbook of Child Psychology,* Worcester, Mass.: Clark University Press, pp. 377-391.

12:43 Piaget, J. (1953). *Psychology and Logic,* London: Manchester University Press.

12:44 Piaget, J. (1950). *The Psychology of Intelligence,* London: Routledge and Kegan Paul. (Especially Ch. 5).

12:45 Piaget, J. (1930). *Immenentisme et for Religieuse,* Geneve: Robert.

12:46 Pixley, E. and E. Beekman (1949). "The Faith of Youth as Shown by a Survey of Public Schools in Los Angeles," *Religious Education,* Vol. 44, pp. 306-342.

12:47 Read, H. (1960). *The Forms of Things Unknown,* New York: Horizon Press.

12:48 Read, H. (1955). *Icon and Idea,* Cambridge, Mass.: Harvard University Press.

12:49 Schilder, P. (1950). *The Image and Appearance of the Human Body,* New York: International Universities Press.

12:50 Spearman, C. (1927). *The Abilities of Man,* London: Macmillan.

12:51 Spearman, C. (1930). *Creative Mind,* London: Cambridge University Press.

12:52 Spilka, B. and J.F. Reynolds. (1965). "Religion and Prejudice: A Factor-Analytic Study," *Review of Religious Research,* 6, pp. 163-168.

12:53 Spilka, B., and M. Mullin. (1974). "Personal Religion and Psycho-Social Schemata: A Research Approach to a Theological Psychology of Religion," Paper presented at convention of the Society for the Scientific Study of Religion, Washington, D.C., October 26, 1974.

12:54 Sully, J. (1907). *Children's Ways,* New York: D. Appleton & Co.

12:55 Tanner, A.E. (1904). *The Child: His Thinking, Feeling, & Doing,* Chicago: Rand McNally & Co.

12:56 Thouless, R.H. (1935). "The Tendency to Certainty in Religious Belief," *British Journal of Psychology,* Vol. 26.

12:57 Tillich, P. (1948). *The Shaking of the Foundations,* New York: Charles Scribner's Sons.

12:58 Torrance, E.P. (1963). *Education and the Creative Potential,* Minneapolis: University of Minnesota Press.

12:59 Vergote, Antoine, (1969). *The Religious Man,* Dublin: Gill and Macmillan.

12:60 Vergote, A. and M. Bonami. (1967). "Le Symbole Paternal, et so Signification Religieuse," in *Archiv fur Religion-psychologie,* Gottingen: Vandenhoeck, pp. 118-140.

12:61 Vernier, C.M. (1952). *Projective Test Productions I. Projective Drawings,* New York: Grune & Stratton.

12:62 Vernon, P.E. (1950). *The Structure of Human Abilities,* London: Methuen.

12:63 Volakova, H. (1964). *I Never Saw Another Butterfly* (a collection of poems & drawings by children in the Terezin Concentration Camp During 1942-1944). New York: McGraw-Hill.

12:64 Wheeler, D.K. (1959). "Symposium: The Development of Moral Values in Children," *British Journal of Educational Psychology,* 29, pp. 118-127.

12:65 Withey, S.P. (1962). "The Influence of the Peer Group on the Value of Youth," *Religious Education* (Supplement), Vol. 57.

AN AUTHOR INDEX

PARZEN, A. (11:14)
PATIFFE, L. (5:57)
PEATLING, J.H. (4:42; 5:58,59,60)
PEEL, E. A. (2:38; 3:51)
PELTZ, R. (10:29)
PENROD, W.T., Jr. (3:52)
PEREZ, M. B. (7:80)
PESCH, C. (4:43)
PIAGET, J. (3:4,33,53,54, 55,56,57,58,59,60,61,62, 63,64; 11:36; 12:42,43, 44,45)
PIXLEY, E. (12:46)
POHIER, J.M. (11:37)
POLE, D. (10:30)
PORTER, K. A. (7:81)
PREUSS, M. (7:28)
PREYER, W. (3:65)
PRITCHETT, K. (3:48)
PROWLLER, W. (7:82)
PRUDHOMMEAU, M. (7:83)

RABELLO, S. (7:84)
RABSON, A. (2:31)
RADKE-YARROW, M. (11:38)
RASKIN, E. (8:5)
READ, H. (10:31; 12:47,48)
REICHARD, S. (2:39)
REICHERT, R. (4:44)
REIK, T. (5:61)
REY, A. (7:85)
REYNOLDS, J.F. (12:52)
RICCI, C. (7:86)
RICHARDS, T.W. (7:55)
RICHARDSON, J.A. (10:32)
ROBINSON, R. (5:62)
ROGOLSKY, M.M. (8:14)
ROLOFF, E. (5:63)
ROONEY, P. (4:35)

ROSENBERG, M.J. (2:1)
ROSENSOHN, M. (1:31,32; 4:46)
ROSS, M.G. (5:64)
ROSSI, P.H. (4:24)
ROSTEN, L. (9:12)
ROUMA, G. (7:87)
RUSSELL, D.H. (2:40)
RUSSELL, T. (7:27)
RYAN, M.P. (5:65)

SALMAN, H.D. (5:66)
SAMUELSON, G. (11:14)
SAVILE, A. (10:33)
SCHAEFFER-SIMMERN, F. (8:15)
SCHALLER, L.E. (9:13)
SCHILDER, P. (12:49)
SCHIUM, M.W. (3:66)
SCHNALL, M. (7:88)
SCHOLL, S.L. (6:20)
SCHURMANS, J. (5:67)
SCHUSSEL, N.R. (10:10)
SCOTT, L. (2:16)
SERRA, M. C. (2:41)
SHERIF, M. (2:42)
SHUTTLEWORTH, F.K. (2:19)
SIEGMAN, A. W. (11:39)
SIGEL, I. E. (3:67)
SIMMONS, A.J. (5:68)
SIMMONS, H. C. (1:28)
SINGER, R. E. (1:29)
SMITH, C.M. (10:34)
SMITH, G. (12:34)
SMITH, G.A. (3:8)
SMITH, J.J. (5:69)
SMITH, J.W.D. (5:70)
SMITHER, E. (4:45)
SMOKE, K.L. (2:43)
SOLLEY, C.M. (2:44)

A JOURNAL INDEX

ALBERTA JOURNAL OF EDUCATIONAL RESEARCH (3:8)
AMERICAN JOURNAL OF ORTHOPSYCHIATRY (2:39; 7:26,42; 8:3)
AMERICAN JOURNAL OF SOCIOLOGY (5:31)
AMERICAN MAGAZINE OF ART (7:9)
AMERICAN PSYCHOLOGIST (5:9; 7:44)
ARCHIV FUER RELIGIONSPSYCHOLOGIE (5:63; 12:60)
ARCHIVES DE PSYCHOLOGIE (7:13,49,66)
ARCHIVES DE PSYCHOLOGIE GENEVA (7:85)
ARCHIVES DE SOCIALOGIE DES RELIGIONS (11:13)
ARCHIVES OF GENERAL PSYCHIATRY (11:14)
ARCHIVES OF PSYCHOLOGY (2:42)
ART BULLETIN (6:19)
ART EDUCATION (7:7, 62, 82; 10:23)

BEHAVIORAL SCIENCE (2:1)
BOLETIN DERETORIA TECN. DE EDUCATION (7:84)
BRITISH JOURNAL OF AESTHETICS (10:28,30,33)
BRITISH JOURNAL OF EDUCATIONAL PSYCHOLOGY (2:38; 12:64)
BRITISH JOURNAL OF PSYCHOLOGY (2:20; 6:1; 10:20; 11:8; 12:56)
BULLETIN OF SOCIAL BINET (8:11)
BULLETIN OF THE UNIVERSITY OF LONDON INSTITUTE OF EDUCATION (12:16)

CHARACTER POTENTIAL: A RECORD OF RESEARCH (3:52; 5:24,58,77; 9:4; 12:22)
CHILD DEVELOPMENT (2:7,8,10,15,16,17,28,31,33,34,36, 50; 3:1,42,44,77; 5:41; 7:20,47,60,68; 11:38; 12:7,39)
CHILD STUDY JOURNAL (7:40)
COLLEGE ART JOURNAL (7:71)

DEVELOPMENTAL PSYCHOLOGY (7:37)

EDUCATION (2:47)
EDUCATION RESEARCH MONTHLY (1:25)
EDUCATIONAL REVIEW (3:9; 7:15; 12:41)

ENFRANCE (7:10)

HUMANITAS (11:20)

INLAND EDUCATOR (7:70)
INSIGHT (11:14)
INTERNATIONAL JOURNAL OF PSYCHOANALYSIS
    (5:51; 11:18)

JAPANESE JOURNAL OF EXPERIMENTAL PSYCHOLOGY
    (7:48)
JOHNS HOPKINS STUDIES IN EDUCATION (12:26)
JOURNAL DE PSYCHOLOGIE NORMALE ET PATHO-
    LOGIQUE (6:17)
JOURNAL FOR THE SCIENTIFIC STUDY OF RELIGION
    (1:4,12; 5:15,17; 11:34,39)
JOURNAL OF ABNORMAL AND SOCIAL PSYCHOLOGY
    (3:47; 10:12)
JOURNAL OF AESTHETIC EDUCATION (10:29,32,34)
JOURNAL OF AESTHETICS AND ART CRITICISM
    (6:2; 10:21,25,35)
JOURNAL O F CONSULTING AND CLINICAL PSYCHOL-
    OGY (7:46,57,61,63; 8:5,6; 10:10)
JOURNAL O F EDUCATIONAL RESEARCH (3:75)
JOURNAL OF EXPERIMENTAL EDUCATION (8:2)
JOURNAL OF EXPERIMENTAL PEDAGOGY (7:4)
JOURNAL OF GENERAL PSYCHOLOGY (10:9)
JOURNAL OF GENETIC PSYCHOLOGY (2:21,35,37;
    3:12,14,15,16,30; 5:12,13,14,42,45,68,71; 7:3,55)
JOURNAL OF GERONTOLOGY (5:11)
JOURNAL OF PROJECTIVE TECHNIQUES (1:20;
    7:39,69,92; 8:14)
JOURNAL OF PSYCHOLOGICAL STUDIES (1:33; 5:8)
JOURNAL OF PSYCHOLOGY (2:24,51; 12:13,14)
JOURNAL OF SCHOOL PSYCHOLOGY (7:28)
JOURNAL OF SOCIAL PSYCHOLOGY (5:39;7:18;11:6,29)
JOURNAL OF THE AMERICAN PSYCHOANALYTIC
    ASSOCIATION (3:19)

LEARNING FOR LIVING (4:18,23,27; 5:2,27,33,34)

UNIVERSITY OF BIRMINGHAM REVIEW (11:28)
UNIVERSITY OF IOWA STUDIES IN CHARACTER (2:2;
   4:4,19; 5:7,32)

ZEITSCHRIFT FUER PEDAGOGISCH PSYCHOLOGIE
   (12:31)